Education for Sustainability

For the first time in human history more people live in the urban rather than the rural environment. We now have to learn to live and flourish in our urban landscape and manage our resources with ecologically informed discretion. Education is going to play a significant role in establishing the conditions for this eco-intelligence.

In this book Paul Clarke, a founding Director and activist of the influential Incredible Edible project, argues that we are functionally ecologically illiterate. We are ignoring the fact that we are destroying our planet and that our existing models of education are contributing to the problem. He maintains that an education that is not grounded in a full understanding of our relationship with the natural world is no education at all. Education is perfectly placed to create the conditions for solutions, and provide the formulas that ensure everyone becomes naturally smart; but to achieve this, a total re-conceptualization of schools and how they serve their communities is needed.

Drawing on innovative sustainable living programmes from around the world, including Sweden's Forest Schools, China's Green Schools programme, the US Green Ribbon Schools programme and his own school-of-sustainability project, Paul Clarke addresses the following 'explorations':

- How do we rethink our relationship with the environment?
- Is education fit for purpose if the purpose is sustainable living?
- How can community help schools to live with uncertainty?
- Open source living – when sustainability is the way of life.
- Can we create schools of sustainability?
- The urban fix: sustainable cities, sustainable minds.

While acknowledging that the ecological crisis is global in scale, Clarke maintains that many of the solutions are already evident within our local communities; a point that is crucial if they are to have a social connectivity that can engage and influence public behaviour. This book opens the door to a new way of imagining how we might proceed with civilization and gives practical ideas about how schools and communities can make their contribution. It is thought provoking, timely, and should be read by anyone involved in child education, policy practice and school management or leadership.

Paul Clarke is a founding Director of the Incredible Edible programme, and Professor of Education at St Mary's University College, London.

Education for Sustainability
Becoming naturally smart

Paul Clarke

Routledge
Taylor & Francis Group

LONDON AND NEW YORK

First published 2012
by Routledge
2 Park Square, Milton Park, Abingdon, Oxon OX14 4RN

Simultaneously published in the USA and Canada
by Routledge
711 Third Avenue, New York, NY 10017

Routledge is an imprint of the Taylor & Francis Group, an informa business

© 2012 Paul Clarke

British Library Cataloguing in Publication Data
A catalogue record for this book is available from the British Library

Library of Congress Cataloging in Publication Data
Clarke, Paul, 1961-
Education for sustainability : becoming naturally smart / by Paul Clarke.
    p. cm.
    Includes bibliographical references and index.
    1. Environmental education.   2. Environmental ethics—Study and teaching.   3. Environmentalism.   4. Public schools.   I. Title.
    GE70.C545 2012
    333.7071—dc23

                                                    2011029344

ISBN: 978-0-415-69871-9 (hbk)
ISBN: 978-0-415-69872-6 (pbk)
ISBN: 978-0-203-13662-1 (ebk)

Typeset in Galliard
by RefineCatch Ltd, Bungay, Suffolk

MIX
Paper from
responsible sources
FSC
www.fsc.org   FSC® C004839

Printed and bound in Great Britain by
TJ International Ltd, Padstow, Cornwall

In loving memory of Chris May

Contents

Figures and tables

Figures

Tables

Acknowledgements

I would like to thank all those who have encouraged and supported me over the many years of thinking and connecting these ideas into a form which you find it today. Special thanks for the encouragement, support and guidance go to Tony Kelly, along with Jane Reed, Tom Are Trippestad, Alys Fowler, Stephen Feber, Chris Cotton, Terry Wrigley, Dave Reynolds, Jim Hewitt, David Hopkins, Mel Ainscow, Mel West and my colleagues at St Mary's University College who have been subjected to my many versions of this story over the past four years. To my children – Alice, Imogen, Isaac and Hannah – for their constant enthusiasm and support of the ideas. I want to make a special mention of thanks to Anna Clarkson for her support, judgment and guidance, I know this project was a leap in the dark, and I hope that what I have managed to do pays off that trust.

I cannot in good conscience give the statutory thanks to my wife, for the helpful comments on the manuscript, patient reading of drafts or corrections in proofs, because Eithne did none of these things. She seldom if ever reads anything I write. Going by the lavish thanks to wives I find in the prefaces to other books, I deem myself uniquely injudicious in having married a woman who refuses to double as a high-grade editorial assistant. Since custom requires me to thank her for something, I thank her for the agreeable fact of her continuing presence which in twenty-five years I have never presumed to expect. [This is paraphrased from the wonderful book by Barbara Trapido: *Brother of the More Famous Jack* (Harmondsworth: Penguin Books, 1998), needless to say passed on to me by Eithne.]

Finally, and sadly. The very day I completed the final Exploration of this book my dear friend and co-conspirator in this work Chris May died. Chris was a continual source of support, challenge and inspiration throughout the writing of this book. We spent many days discussing the themes and ideas that are covered in the pages here. I feel incredibly privileged that he wanted to work on this project with me, spending time to not just reading, but making copious notes of the drafts I put in his direction, which he would then go through forensically, questioning and clarifying, and inevitably improving. I loved his playful intelligence, humour and razor-sharp clarity, qualities which make for wonderful company. Not to be able to have those moments any more with my friend is like having a window blocked up on the world, but it also makes those moments we spent working, laughing and playing together even more precious. I hope, in concluding the work without Chris to probe, prompt and push, that it lives up to his expectations.

Foreword
Growing communities

In my twenties I worked as a gardener for five years. It was joyous but hard work. In 1987 I became a primary school teacher in Bristol. Working in early-years settings convinced me that gardening, food production and cooking could act as a basis for pretty much all learning in the primary curriculum, as the children were utterly enthused and absorbed when they were practically engaged in these life-affirming pursuits, and learned effortlessly, their creativity and curiosity constantly stimulated and nourished by the natural world around them. What's more, gardening made them happy and they loved learning outdoors. Dismayed with the educational policies of the 80s and 90s, like so many others who loved teaching but disliked schools, I left teaching and pursued different paths.

It is hugely exciting now to see that ideas about food, the environment and learning are permeating the educational landscape with renewed energy and vigour. It has been a great privilege to meet up regularly with my friend Paul Clarke to discuss this new book. I've been sharing ideas with Paul for the last year or so and it has been a fascinating ongoing discussion, as there are so many resonances between his ideas for developing sustainable learning communities and the work to recognise the value of schools as hubs for community capacity building through creativity and culture.

Paul is as passionate as it gets about the need to address the crisis that is staring us in the face. Put simply, we cannot go on ignoring the fact that we are destroying our planet and in the process are holding onto a model of education that is contributing to unsustainability. Paul suggests we need to develop radical solutions to address our foolish addiction to progress through consumerism, and our short-sighted adherence to the idea that inexorable growth is the solution. The answer, he says, is to rethink our relationship with the environment and to totally rethink our concept of schools.

What I love about this work is its radicalism. Paul doesn't hold back from suggesting a total redesign of the ways in which schools work, and his vision for schools as the core of community renaissance programmes that emphasise the need for all learning to be grounded in a full appreciation of environmental action which starts with the growing of food, is compelling. The book is full of detailed and careful thinking about both why we have to act and how we might move forwards. The inspirational community gardening and learning initiative – Incredible Edible – based where Paul lives in Todmorden (and of which Paul is a founding member) is referenced as an effective model for community capacity building that is demonstrating the power of these ideas when they are realised in action.

Paul's ideas make absolute sense to me and I look forward to exploring further how we can work together to test them in practice with our school partners and in other settings. My own view is that we should take a hard look at the sort of growth we should aspire to as a society. Study after study would seem to reveal that the relentless pursuit of material growth produces no overall improvements in people's happiness or well-being; in fact the opposite seems true. So let's aim for a growth in social justice, growth in mental well-being, growth in community cohesion and growth in imagination and spirit as a set of aims.

I'm confident enough about the power of these ideas to make a prediction that in 20 years' time it will be inconceivable for a school, wherever it is located, to be built without the inclusion of a food production and energy generation system that is fully integrated into both the fabric of the building and the fabric of the curriculum. We'll look back at these risk-averse times, where children spend ridiculous amounts of time shut up inside schools, missing out on the limitless opportunities presented by learning in the outdoors, as being truly absurd. We'll eventually come to our senses and realise that an education that is not grounded in a full understanding of our environment and how we can build a sustainable future together is no education at all. In writing this book, Paul has opened the door to a new way of imagining how we might proceed with civilization; this is a massive achievement and a very important and timely piece of work.

Chris May
April 2011

Prologue
Imagine an alternative

> Teacher: *Which came first, the chicken or the egg?*
> Child: *A duck.*

One of the most commercially successful and long-standing children's confectionaries sold around the world is the Kinder Egg, or Kinder Surprise. The Kinder Surprise originated in 1972 and is a global phenomenon, manufactured under franchise by many companies worldwide (see http://www.magic-kinder.com). The confectionary consists of an outside aluminum wrapper, a chocolate candy egg, and a small toy that has to be assembled. The toy is usually made of plastic, but occasionally of tin, and it is often designed by commissioned artists. The Kinder Eggs are sold all over the world with the exclusion of United States, where the 1938 Federal Food, Drug, and Cosmetic Act prohibits embedding 'non-nutritive items' in confectionary.

In Europe, their popularity has spread beyond their intended market of children and the eggs have become a cult item among adults. There is a thriving collectors' market for the Kinder toys. This is especially true in Germany, where the manufacturer includes higher-quality toys than are available elsewhere. There are many types of toys available, but some of the most popular with collectors include the constantly revised series of small hand-painted figures (some have to be assembled), which are said to be in every seventh egg; cartoon characters; metal figures; and jigsaw puzzles. Seasonal eggs are introduced around the holiday periods, such as the limited-edition nativity collections (featuring such characters as the three kings, baby Jesus, and assorted farmyard animals) found around Christmas, and the huge ones found at Easter (extremely popular in Italy). A relatively new innovation, adding to the product and triggered by the advent of the Internet, is the introduction of 'Internet surprises'. Accompanying the toy is a small slip of paper containing a 'Magicode'. This code gives access to games at the Magic Kinder website; some for downloading and others for playing online.

Kinder Eggs illustrate the first part of our story of our modern world in microcosm, they epitomize what I am going to describe as ecological blindness and urban industrialism. This blindness is a consequence of a particular way in which products are made. Their design is structured around the model of take, make and dump. Essentially the product is conceived as a disposable commodity, and this process is evident from start to finish. The eggs are a global phenomenon; due to licensing arrangements and distribution networks and through their manufacturing processes the eggs literally travel the world, their waste is therefore globally distributed. At the same time, they are now also a virtual product, due to their post-production processing, where their owners can extend the experience of purchasing the egg through the multi-lingual websites, game sites, and collectors sites, enticing them to buy more, collect more, spend more, consume more. The product is a complex story of composites, ranging from material extraction, to creative design. The physical product is a combination of an aluminum wrapper (the majority of which is mined in Australia), chocolate (in the case of the egg I am looking at made in the UK, a plastic toy [made in China] and a set of instructions [paper of unknown origin printed in Belgium]), and it costs 58p (just about US$1) in the sweet shop. The gratification of the chocolate may be relatively short lived, but the physical presence of the product's packaging, which could quite likely end up in a landfill site, takes up to 250 years to decompose.

At first glance the modest apple could not be more different from the Kinder Egg. It is a natural product and, once eaten, its remains will rot and decompose within a few weeks. But what we see as a fruit is not necessarily what it represents as a product.

The apple is also the result of considerable human intervention and design. The apple is one of the most widely cultivated tree fruits on the planet, and the most widely known of the many members of genus *Malus* that are used by humans. The apple tree originated from Western Asia, where its wild ancestor is still found today. There are more than 7,500 known varieties of apples, resulting in a range of desired characteristics. Cultivars vary in their yield and the ultimate size of the tree, even when grown on the same rootstock. Apples represent big business. At least 55 million tonnes of apples were grown worldwide in 2005, with a value of about US$10 billion. China produced about 35 per cent of this total; the United States is the second-leading producer, with more than 7.5 per cent of world production; Iran is third, followed by Turkey, Russia, Italy and India.

The apple tree is thought to be the earliest tree to be cultivated by humans, and its fruits have been improved through selection over thousands of years. Alexander the Great is credited with finding dwarfed apples in Asia Minor in 300 BCE; those he brought back to Macedonia might have been the progenitors of dwarfing rootstocks. Winter apples, picked in late autumn and stored just above freezing, have been an important food in Asia and Europe for millennia, as well as in Argentina and in the United States since the arrival of Europeans. Apples were brought to North America with colonists in the seventeenth century, and the first apple orchard on the North American continent was said to be near Boston in 1625. In the twentieth century, irrigation projects in Washington State began and allowed the development of the multibillion dollar fruit industry, of which the apple is the leading species. Modern apple farm production demands considerable land space, fertilizer and pesticides, as well as physical management and movement of the product from farm to plate.

Different worlds, one story

The Kinder Egg and the apple both converge on the central theme of this book; it is through the small, day-to-day repetitive actions that we are now entirely urban in our outlook. The distinction between urban and rural no longer prevails – all is urban. And because our entire way of being is urban, I think we have to begin to learn how to ensure that the natural is part of our urban, and the unnatural, the downside of the designs for life such as the Kinder Egg, are eliminated or radically modified to fit in with our new ways of doing business.

The Kinder Egg and the apple suggest that what is considered to be natural and what is man-made are not perhaps as clear-cut as we have grown accustomed to assume; we are intertwined with that which is natural. While we see the clear role that we have in the production of the Kinder Egg, when we see the apple we perhaps miss many of the same production-based techniques that are systemically spread like a mycelium throughout the modern world. The growing of the apple is one thing, but where it ends up is an entirely different story. Such is our modern reality; we live in a post-production world where nothing is quite as it might first appear.

We didn't perhaps plan for these circumstances to occur. But when repeated on a global scale, the consequences of what we are doing become tragic and increasingly toxic. One Kinder Egg at a time might look benign, but globally they add up to a huge pile of toxic plastic waste. Similarly, one poorly educated, industrialized learner adds a lifetime of human toxicity to the already huge pile. Magnify this from the singular example of the egg or the apple and apply it to the entire production of human activity and it becomes very clear what is happening. We are working to a fundamentally defective plan; it is strategically and systemically tragic. If we claim, as I do, that we consciously plan for change and find ourselves arguing that we didn't plan for these detrimental environmental things to happen, we are still complicit in contributing to the problem; it is no excuse to claim that we didn't know what we were doing.

This broad quest for how to act today, *how to live, how to be, to think, to do*, thus serves as our script, a story for our time. It is through just such questions that a counter-cultural narrative has emerged on a global level. This widespread and dispersed set of narratives that examine alternatives to the mainstream are creating the fault line in the conventional story, busting the myth of consumer growth and economic progress, it opens us up to the possibility of new rhetorical positions based upon a new reading of how to live sustainably.

Finding the new balance with Nature, a balance that restores our place in the Natural order of things, is to ensure we instruct wisely as we tell our stories, a theme I will explore further in these pages.

Introduction

In the 1970s, Educational Effectiveness Research stood against the currents of the time, intellectually and politically. Maybe it needs to rediscover that radical spirit again, in this and in other areas related to the future of international society.

Reynolds et al. 2011

In 2010, the human race changed from being predominantly rural to predominantly urban. We can now legitimately claim to be an industrial, human-centric, urban species. This industrialization shapes our economies, our societies and our cultures, and its lexicon of improvement and effectiveness determines how we collectively think and act. More than 3.3 billion people now live in urban environments; by 2030 this is estimated to increase to 5 billion of a global population predicted to peak at around 9 billion mid-century (UN Population predictions 2010). The dominant narrative of the modern urban world, which forms many of the conditions in the cities we inhabit globally, has emerged from the industrial era, and this narrative is promoted and maintained through an overwhelmingly industrial model of schooling. However, its utilitarianism is showing signs of fatigue; simultaneously with the rise in population, we are witnessing an unprecedented collapse in our global ecosystem and increasing dysfunction in our systems of education, health, politics, finance and agriculture. The established linear capitalist model seems no longer sufficient to provide for a changing reality, which suggests that the way we relate to our world is outdated, destructive and unsustainable, and our solutions predictable, short-term and pathologically selfish.

What happens next? This largely depends upon how, and whether, we can we learn to live more sustainably in our built landscapes and communities around the planet, turning our collective genius for science, technology and the arts towards establishing new foundations for a sustainable society. This is ultimately an educational challenge; a challenge of how to respond to a crisis through schooling in its broadest sense and with practical sustainable solutions.

In the coming years our international society is going to have to come to terms with learning a new language of togetherness. This recent transition from the rural to the urban represents a significant moment not just for us in our urban world, but also for what has been called until now, the natural world. What will our relationship with our world look like in the twenty-first century, and is our orchestration of urban life sufficiently responsive to the natural environment, or is it predominantly human-centric?

A measure of our action

As we settle in to our new-found urban mind, what will be the measure of our collective action? We already have some indicators: for industrialized nations the sum of our activity currently boils down to Gross National Product (GNP), an economic metric; in the Kingdom of Bhutan, the sum of collective worth is measured as Gross National Happiness, a measure of well-being; in China, the government has recently announced a national Talent Plan,[1] a skills measure. Yet while these different measures are important, they are trumped by one single overarching value which functions universally as a coherent measure of concern: that of ecological sustainability,[2] a life-ensuring measure. All other measures – indeed all other endeavours, whether technological, scientific, artistic or economic – are reduced to nothing if the ecological systems upon which we depend cease to function (Berry 2005). It therefore becomes the significant educational question: how do we educate and school ourselves as a species in order to establish the conditions which are conducive to maintaining life on earth? It is not something we have yet established as a basis for our educational actions and, consequently, our trajectory of development has been and remains fundamentally unsustainable. As we have sought greater literacy in the traditional sense, we have become functionally illiterate ecologically. We need a radical rediscovery of our educational purpose, a renaissance of the educational enterprise for our urban age.

This is therefore a book about the emergence of a culture of connection and ecological emergence. Whereas industrialized modern life has flourished by fragmenting our world-view, an approach that has enabled us to understand in great detail the sum of the parts, it has led us into a cul-de-sac when we try to make sense of the whole. If we are to take a substantive step forward with our appreciation of the ecological, we have to renew our understanding and relationship with the entire earth system, re-culturing for the time we live in. In this work I am therefore looking for ways in which schools and communities might achieve this and reconnect to ideas, to action, to place and to each other. The reason for this interest lies in my starting question: What is the measure of our collective action, and does it suit our collective urbanized purpose? What emerges from the question is summed up in the need for a redefinition of collective purpose and practice. It is absolutely possible that we can change, and absolutely possible that urban life will enhance rather than negate our relationship with the natural world. This book is therefore drafted as a search for a way of living sustainably, which requires us to consider basic needs, to look again at what we have, and to fashion a way forward that is in keeping with our intentions while recognizing that we have a great propensity to delude and deceive ourselves about what we do. Our guide needs to be wiser than we are, and we suggest that guide is nature, or perhaps more poetically we might consider our guide to be the conditions that are conducive to life (Wilson 2002).

To regain that connection we have to experiment and break rank from the consensus, because only through experimentation and innovation can we witness new examples and provide new direction – example and direction are two critical elements that any transition requires to move from one set of circumstances to another. In any transition we will make mistakes as well as breakthroughs. The type of societal organization that is required has to cope with failure as well as success, and this is different from the type of social system we have engineered to manage with today's world. Instead of a no-fail model, we need to establish the conditions where failure is understood as part of an evolutionary process, but is then used productively to inform and guide our next efforts.

We are not talking here about systems that require absolutes. Despite the circumstances being urgent if not critical, we must continue to explore and create new solutions and not resort to existing formulations or restrictive visions of the possible, as these will not generate the transformational capabilities we require to overcome the ecological conditions we face. After all, we are talking about human systems of community, relationship to each other and to place, to ideas and to actions, and these are slow to change. We need to learn how to live together within this period of uncertainty, how to draw upon our qualities of resourcefulness and resilience to chart new ways of understanding, new ways of engaging with, and foster new ways of living in our world, as it exists now, which will serve us as starting points in the journey to what might become a more sustainable future. To do this, we have to create a capability to deal with uncertainty of solutions, it has to be just as robust a way of living as the one we have created that manages the conditions of certainty.

We have pursued the 'modern experiment' for the past few hundred years, it is an experiment which has established a powerful narrative of self (Clarke 2000). Success is not seen in the round, as a set of systemic conditions that are individually successful but recognizably interdependent. Instead, success is based upon getting ahead of the crowd, it is individualized and egocentric (Kumar 2002).

On a broader, cultural level, this narrative plays itself out in the way that we have designed our living spaces. These see how far we can go on our own, to the exclusion of all other life on earth. Witness the anonymous, glass boxes that continue to be built in our cities all around the world. They are undeniably remarkable feats of engineering but they exclude; they use huge amounts of energy; they have no truck with any connection with the natural environment; they represent a way of thinking that is well past its sell by date; a selfish, egotistical course which has led towards an increasingly human-centric world – but there are signs of change. London, for example, has a long history of food growing in allotments and community growing schemes; across the city the demand for these growing spaces has never been higher. Paris is currently undergoing a rooftop bee-keeping revolution which is rebuilding what was once present across the skyline of the city, but was curtailed because of the Second World War and fell out of fashion in the 1950s. Vancouver is getting considerable attention worldwide for its urban design, and the ways in which community food growing has flourished in the urban inner city in recent years. Likewise, we see examples in the New York city rooftop gardens, and the Havana project in Cuba has an international following because of the way that the farmers have established themselves again as a vital component of the communities in which they grow.

We can see the modern legacy all around us, but most poignantly we witness it in our cities, where we have until recently almost entirely eliminated the basic stuff of life – food. Despite the pioneering examples, modern urban designers have conceived cities not as places of life sustaining practice, but business sustaining practice. Consequently, we have divorced and distanced ourselves in our cities from a fundamental life source – food. With food comes other life; the biodiversity of insects, birds, and plants (Wilson 1991). By creating the modern city in the manner that we have chosen, we are crushing our connection with life.

We have become more and more dependent upon our sophisticated systems that connect globally to provide us with our foods, and as we do that we grow ever more vulnerable (Steel 2009). It is also, ultimately, both a lonely and a finite course to adopt, lacking vitality, harmony and comfort that comes from being among beings other than ourselves; finite because the energy resources we rely upon to move that food are themselves running lower each year.

As this modern experiment shows increasing signs of fatigue, and as an older order of things starts to decay, we begin to see glimpses of the emergence of new ideas about how to proceed. These ideas examine places, interests, relationships, actions all leading to renewed thinking about how we might live and act out our lives in a different way (Clarke 2009a). If we take time to reflect on the results of the modern human experiment of the past two to three hundred years since the industrial revolution, we might conclude that it has been a mixed success; we have managed to do some amazing things, and we have also managed to get ourselves into a complete mess.

I intend to weave a narrative that examines how we might learn from where we are, and usefully adopt and adapt to a new set of conditions. These are at best the formative conditions of a design for living, perhaps that form of living might be more informed and adopt practices that are sustainable. As such, our story here is not an end in itself; far from it. It merely sketches possible ways forward. It recognizes that there is a powerful history of talent and creativity upon which we can now build and evolve to a new phase of human activity on earth. It asks, for example, how might we turn the genius that has established modern consciousness with all the science, technology and arts towards establishing the new foundations for a sustainable society? It recognizes that the most important resources available to us are our creativity and imagination, because they enable us to conceive that which is not yet realized. We are at a point in history where our technologies, our sciences and our arts have all demonstrated the power of human imagination and ambition; it is as if we are a collective body of ever-evolving ideas and solutions, an interconnected global pulse of possibility. I want to suggest that we can choose to harness this power and focus on the critical challenges of our time through a revised process of enlightened public education. It is a selfless choice, an infinite choice, and a choice of, and for, permanence. We can move there if we choose to see the world through a new lens of sustainable growth and life. And if we consider this as possible, we soon recognize that we need to establish a new language of practice to inform and guide our activity.

There are three basic conditions which will provide a starting point for educating for sustainability:

1   We need to establish the understanding of why and how we care for our planet, the only one we have.
2   We need to understand the need to care for each other, so we can live harmoniously.
3   We need to understand that there is a need to care for ourselves, which includes self-discipline to learn to have what we need and not always what we want; this means redesigning our consumption to meet the demands of the other two conditions.

We know that we hold an immense responsibility in our hands to pass on to our children the necessary knowledge, skills and understanding to ensure that they are both capable and competent to live their lives on the earth in a responsible and caring manner, confident in the knowledge that their actions ensure that their children will inherit a place that is better equipped to sustain and provide abundant facility for life.

Two critical components of this knowledge and understanding come through robust relationships with the natural world, and with each other; relationships that are founded upon an in-depth knowledge of what we mean by permanence. An ecologically sustainable world is predicated upon the interconnection of ourselves with the entire web of life (Holzer 2010). If we lose our connection with the earth we forget we are of the earth, we begin to fabricate an illusion of our own importance alongside the larger presence of our planet. We have to include these ideas within all of our systems and organizations as common and core values and principles of operation. This needs to be the modus operandi of global human action.

We have therefore pursued the simple idea that a revised form of education might play a transformational role in cultivating a cultural change towards this more sustainable way of living, thereby providing us with a clearer sense of direction.

I will suggest that to get to a new consciousness we have to discover new ways to solve our problems. We need to explore the way that we might think and act in response to our growing understanding of the influence that the natural world has on our own way of being and doing. I also want to point out that this is an immediate need, and not something that can be pitched forward as 'education for the future'. The pressing demands of a changing climate have made the issue both urgent and contemporary. To think about sustainability as something that we can neatly package and develop for tomorrow is to miss the point; we deal with our unsustainable present, and through doing this we educate for sustainability for now, which in turn makes tomorrow a slightly less difficult prospect. That is why growing is such a useful metaphor. We plant a seed, an idea, it needs to be nurtured and maintained and provided with the conditions to ensure it will flourish, and in turn, over time, it becomes a mature plant or tree, or an established cultural norm or practice. It doesn't just happen overnight but, in turn, it has to begin now, or else we have nothing to come to fruition. The notion of growing from within has long been associated with the quest for learning, while growing in a physical sense concerns transitions from birth, to child, to youth, to adult and ultimately to death. We transcend our own demise by passing on knowledge and understanding to the next generation, we extend our reach inter-generationally. It also has educational and schooling implications by which we can pass ecological wisdom from generation to generation into the future. But this is a delicate and conscious act of informed judgment, an act of fine, intelligent balance. This cycle of life is universal; it extends from every one of us to the entire biological community of which we are a part. As we grow we learn, what we learn therefore serves to define us.

It was in my years as a teacher that I formed the basis of my understanding of the importance of learning about natural systems and how the school environment could serve as a powerful foundation for an understanding of what it is to live sustainably. Children, I find, have a very direct and practical affinity to the natural world; it is somewhere to play, to discover, and to learn. When I moved to work in the University sector and got involved in work that included the design and development of school networks and systems reform through School Effectiveness and School Improvement research, I maintained a view, which was not prevalent at the time and perhaps remains contentious, that education has to provide the architecture of mind that mimics what we understand from the fundamentals of natural systems if we are to succeed in establishing true learning communities; namely, that nothing is permanent, nothing is fixed, everything is emergent and evolving. If our systems and structures manage to capture just a fraction of the essence of this reality, then we begin to generate educational approaches and designs that are truly emancipatory and radical groundings for people to break out of the existing modes of thinking and living and move into sustainable solutions. The same underlying thread of ideas has persisted into my present profile of work, both in the grounded activity of the Incredible Edible project, the School of Sustainability blog (http://www.school-of-sustainability.com) and the Pop-Up-Farm projects – talking and planning with many community growing projects in the UK and worldwide, and working within a global corporation to support the human infrastructure reforms that are becoming increasingly necessary to compensate for, and to respond to, a rapidly changing global ecological crisis. While the dominant form of education that is provided by our schools remains restrictive and frequently fails to embrace anything other than mainstream thinking, I have grown increasingly encouraged by the evidence that the status quo is breaking down, and we are beginning to witness a renaissance of ideas about the possible ways that schools can be reinvented for a new ecologically defined era. A school plays a critical part in this process of enlightenment. School can play an equally important part in providing a cultural barometer for the next steps we take. For example, schools are important points of contact within communities, but these contacts are often rather fragile and temporary. However, if we were to use a connector, such as food, and introduce this into the centre of the school community as a means of engaging students, teachers, parents and grandparents, we suddenly discover a whole new level of possible ways that school can provide a community with resource, guidance, ideas and opportunities that helps us all to make cities better places in which to live. This is, in my mind, the real meaning of school improvement, it is a radical reappraisal of the current managerial formulation of 'improvement' that has defined policy and practice for the past two decades, and a departure into new territory connecting hand, heart and mind.

The examples here describe how the act of growing food can transform human relationship with place:

- to establish new forms of creativity (from a physical relationship with the land through growing food, to the conceptual puzzles of how to establish suitable methodologies for abundant and ecologically sustainable production);
- to the management and enhancement of knowledge, design and management of complex growing sites through permaculture and its associated principles, the structural and engineering challenges of designing and building hydroponic growing spaces suited to urban contexts;
- to the adoption of new governance models such as community interest companies and new funding schemes that can ensure long-term economic viability of the projects.

In every example we see that schools that adopt a growing community concept can completely change how they interpret, understand, relate to and use their public spaces, change their relationship with their local community, and play a significant strategic role in the long-term security of food in their locality; providing others around them with ways of seeing how to re-imagine their lives for a more sustainable form of community. We learn that we have to know how to nurture our growing produce; we develop specific, contextualized understanding of our relationship to each other, and to the soil, water, plants, light, heat and the ways they all combine to ensure the conditions conducive to life. These simple starting points provide our students and citizens with a direct link to their environment and offer them a route to redefine their urban environments based upon what they discover. They are the first steps towards an eco-capability, they represent ways of thinking that break the centuries-old boundary of urban and rural, city and country, and instead they recognize that we are in nature everywhere – we just have to begin to make sure that nature is in us.

This learning extends the existing notion of school to breaking point, it challenges us to reform school for our time, and reform how we think about school, what it teaches, how it teaches, who it teaches, and where it teaches.[3] It places education and schooling at the heart of a new agenda, an eco-literate agenda, where the educational focus is on the practicalities of neighbourhood renewal, community regeneration, business linking, start-up projects. From community we create town, then city, then megacity; the pattern recurs but the basic ideas remain robust – life ensuring, life enhancing. This is the significance of educational effectiveness and improvement for the transformation of schools, it signifies a step-change from the earlier formulation of the field (Reynolds *et al.* 2011).

I will illustrate how our school communities can play a part in balancing the demands of both self-reliance and interdependence. I will consider some of the capabilities inherent in how people can learn to live sustainably and embed such capabilities into daily life.

The book also concurs with the idea that much of what we do is governed by powerful synthesis of cultural, economic and political narratives (Clarke 2010c). Narratives are important for our understanding, but they are not always consistent nor are they entirely coherent; their power lies perhaps in the overlap of interests, actions, place and relationship, all of which can change over time. Narratives are in effect explorations, devices that can be used to examine – both in the form of reportage and whimsy – the possibilities that are open to any situation.

In writing this book, I have grown increasingly aware that in a period of transition this overlap of similarly conceived, but differently configured, responses to the presenting world is important, as it is the weave of what makes a community connect and learn and evolve. However, it poses a problem for the particular narrative evident in this book – the work is inevitably, and almost forever, unfinished. Indeed, I put aside the equivalent of an entire manuscript because I felt that the lived experience of the story had overtaken the telling. For example, there is such a vast arena of work to connect under the sustainability narrative that any traditional sequential narrative that leads to conclusive claims is rendered ludicrous. To tackle this stylistic problem, I have come to the view that this book is perhaps best read as a set of loosely connected thought pieces – or as I have described, Explorations – set into as coherent a sequence as I could establish. Bertold Brecht was famous for his montages, a series of divergent episodes which have some degree of connection but in turn are in themselves coherent pieces. The aim here is not to claim or to establish any overall coherence, as we are not yet in a position to suggest that what the book examines is in any way coherently conceived. Instead, I want to indicate that there is a need to explore, and to explore the possibilities that are currently in front of us is to generate a new dialogue, a new realism for our time. This is, I suggest, the challenge that every one of us faces in living within an unsustainable world and, while aspiring for the opposite, we have to dream and imagine in order to develop, but we do so with our feet rooted in the reality of the now, recognizing that the fragmentation we encounter in daily life is our current reality, but also recognizing that we can move forward and learn to understand otherwise.

To examine this subject matter, the book is structured around a set of Explorations. They are exploratory because in each the ideas examine some, but not all, of the ways we might consider, contextualize, review and respond to issues that concern sustainability and education. Each chapter is defined in the form of an Exploration and attempts to provide a perspective upon various aspects of the contemporary problem, beginning with challenges we know about, and leading towards a range of ways in which we might usefully respond.

Exploration One: Rethinking our relationship with the environment

In order to build upon any notion of sustainable living we need to understand why there is a need to move in this direction. This Exploration attempts to contextualize the argument for sustainable action by considering the pressing challenges humankind faces this century. The chapter serves as a backdrop to the rest of the book, first by identifying the reasons why there are efforts being made to address climate change, and then to examine the mechanism of sustainable practice, and why such efforts are proving to be problematic. Finally, we will consider the reasons why education will play such an important role in defining and addressing such challenges.

Exploration Two: An investigation of the educational response to ecological challenge

In this Exploration, I will argue that the dominant story of our time, which promotes a view of progress through industrial growth, is no longer tenable if we are to establish a sustainable system of living. In challenging this view, we encounter not only the infrastructure of the industrial era, but also the industrial mind. Consequently, our collective human ego that is manifested in the structures and systems of modernism represent a significant force to contend with if we are to transcend current problems and formulate new ways of thinking. Our future lies in overcoming this human system, moving our action from ego to eco – to become Naturally Smart.

Exploration Three: How can community help schools to live with uncertainty?

If a new social design is to emerge, then the nature of the connections we establish at a local level begin to matter a great deal, as these will either enable or inhibit risk taking. We know that community can serve as a powerful mechanism of support in times of change. This Exploration will discuss some of the ways we might think about the ways that community maintains strong relationships of trust and self-reliance.

Exploration Four: Open source living: when sustainability is the way of life

This Exploration will look at recent trends emerging from what might best be described as social consumerism, experiments in new forms of shared, leased ownership, and open-source thinking arising from a networked society. It will describe in some detail the Incredible Edible project, and explain why a project, which at first sight could be thought of as a community growing project, actually serves as a Trojan Horse for a much more substantive way of thinking about sustainable living, taking the argument from the lifestyle choice to a way of living.

Exploration Five: Can we create schools of sustainability?

We need communities willing to embrace changes in their practice, this means communities that will take risks and learn new behaviour. To do this we have to consider how we re-educate the urban mind, and we use the dominant community learning facility – the school – to explore the way we see that this urban mind can be influenced through its demonstrable actions and leadership. This takes us beyond our current idea of school, into a renaissance of a school for, or of, sustainability.

Exploration Six: The urban fix: sustainable cities, sustainable minds

John Ruskin spoke to an age that was in the formative stages of urbanizing, and successfully established an illusion of the relationship between nature and ourselves that remains to this day. While he foresaw and forewarned of many of the potential challenges that humankind would face as a result of urban life, nothing could have prepared him for the current challenge we face at the start of the twenty-first century, and the environmental crisis we are watching unfold. Here I argue that we need to connect the rural and the urban, conceptually and practically.

Exploration Seven: Our great work: education for sustainability

In the final Exploration, I contextualize my work within what Thomas Berry called *The Great Work* (Berry 1999, 2009). This provides a focus for what we, as educators, must attend to as our primary activity in the coming years as we respond to the question: How do we create and grow sustainable learning communities?

Notes

1 Measure of a country's total economic activity, or the wealth of the country. GNP is usually assessed quarterly or yearly, and is defined as the total value of all goods and services produced by firms owned by the country concerned. It is measured as the gross domestic product plus income earned by domestic residents from foreign investments, minus income earned during the same period by foreign investors in the country's domestic market. GNP does not allow for inflation or for the overall value of production. It is an important indicator of an economy's strength (Hussain 2009).

The *National Medium- and Long-term Talent Development Plan (2010–2020)* creates a blueprint for creating a highly skilled national work force within the next 10 years. This plan is the first major national comprehensive plan in China's history of national human resources development since the Cultural Revolution and is of vital importance to China's current and future development in the next decade and beyond. In Chinese, the plan refers to the development of *rencai*, which can be translated as educated and skilled individuals. Source http://www.brookings.edu/papers/2010/1123_china_talent_wang.aspx (last accessed on 14/12/2010).

2 Ecological Sustainability: To be maintained, the diversity of life and the basis of its productivity must not be systematically diminished, and must be restored where it has been diminished.

3 This idea draws upon a long tradition of dissenting voices in the educational field, and of particular significance is the work of Reimer (1971) and Illich and Verne (1976).

Exploration One

Rethinking our relationship with the environment

I think that there are good reasons for suggesting that the modern age has ended. Today, many things indicate that we are going through a transitional period when it seems that something else is painfully being born. It is as if something were crumbling, decaying, and exhausting itself – while something else, still indistinct, were rising from the rubble.

Vaclev Havel, President Czech republic, speech in Philadelphia, June 1994

The accumulation of human activity over the past 200 or so years has begun to mount up in an unsustainable manner and we are starting to realize that we need to do something about it. Our collective ways of living are starting to cause us real problems. The question is, are we too late to save ourselves?

Stewart Brand (2009), a veteran commentator of environment and sustainable living, defines the problem in terms of three forces:

1   Scale – planetary.
2   Scope – centuries.
3   Stakes – civilization.

He contextualizes these three forces within the self-accelerating human technologies and the growing climatic turbulence. Brand characteristically says that talk of saving the planet is overstated: 'Earth will be fine, no matter what; so will life. It is humans who are in trouble. But since we got ourselves into this fix, we should be able to get ourselves out of it' (ibid., p. 2).

This notion of an impending global crisis is not founded on a fanciful daydream, it is built on a disturbing set of facts. The prospects for human life on earth at the end of the century on an equivalent scale to that of today are becoming extremely unlikely given current climate projections, and especially if in addition we continue to deplete the natural resources in such an unabated fashion. We are in what the renowned biologist E. O. Wilson describes as a bottleneck, where demand is continually outstripping supply across the planet. He writes:

> Everyone can, in theory at least, be housed and fed, but the pressures on the last remnants of wild biodiversity might easily grow fatal for a majority of the remaining ecosystems and their distressed plants and animals. The only way to carry biodiversity safely through the bottleneck of this critical period is by a combination of scientific and technological innovation, abatement of population growth, and environmental education, guided by redirection of moral purpose.
>
> (Wilson 2002: viii)

The form of response will also be dictated not by ourselves but by nature, as climate change begins to have an influence through the increased likelihood of flooding, soil erosion, desertification and drought. The projected increase in temperature around the planet suggests that many of us face a very different kind of future when compared with the world we recognize at present – but what might that future be like?

Sustainable retreat?

This is the fundamental challenge we face against the reality of a warming planet; how do we get ourselves out of this mess? Crudely, the rationale is as follows: as the planet heats up, the ground conditions get warmer. In what is called a positive feedback loop where a particular set of circumstances reinforce themselves on a particular trajectory, white ice reflects sunlight at a rate of 85 per cent, while the dark ocean only reflects 5 per cent; this ensures a balance between heat and cool (see Santer 1996, 2003). However, add in greater levels of heat and we get less ice, which in turn means more absorption of solar heat, which leads to less ice – the result being positive feedback where the system responds to perturbation in the same direction as the original perturbation. But it doesn't stop there. Increasing temperature leads to melting tundra. This melting of permafrost releases vast amounts of methane, a super-greenhouse gas, as a result of the previously frozen vegetation rotting away. More melting of permafrost leads to more greenhouse gas – another positive feedback. In the oceans we face similar problems; 14°C sees the emergence of surface stratification, and this process keeps cold water nutrients out of the reach of sunlight (White and White 2006). The result is that algae cannot grow and vast areas of oceans become effectively dead, their carbon-fixing capacities no longer function. Currently, we estimate that oceans absorb a third of the CO_2 emissions we generate; if we disable the carbon-fixing capacity of the oceans, we turn the natural solution to a natural problem (Hegerl 1996). This we know. What we do not know as yet is the tipping point.

John Beddington, the UK Government's Chief Scientific Adviser, recently warned of extremely difficult times ahead, to which government needed to begin to respond; where climate change, energy shortages, food shortages and water depletion all converge to create the 'perfect storm of environmental and economic collapse' (Beddington 2009). The Intergovernmental Panel on Climate Change (IPCC) reported in its final section on observed changes in climate in their global review as follows:

- Warming of the climate system is unequivocal, as is now evident from observations of increases in global average air and ocean temperatures, widespread melting of snow and ice and rising global average sea level.
- Many natural systems, on all continents and in some oceans, are being affected by regional climate changes. Observed changes in many physical and biological systems are consistent with warming. As a result of the uptake of anthropogenic (human generated) CO_2 since 1750, the acidity of the surface ocean has increased.
- Global total annual anthropogenic GHG emissions,[1] weighted by their 100-year GWPs,[2] have grown by 70 per cent between 1970 and 2004. As a result of anthropogenic emissions, atmospheric concentrations of nitrous oxide now far exceed pre-industrial values spanning many thousands of years, and those of methane and carbon dioxide now far exceed the natural range over the last 650,000 years (Ramaswamy 2006).
- Most of the global average warming over the past 50 years is very likely due to anthropogenic greenhouse gas increases and it is likely that there is a discernible human-induced warming averaged over each continent (except Antarctica).
- Anthropogenic warming over the past three decades has likely had a discernible influence at the global scale on observed changes in many physical and biological systems (Peterson 2008).

Daily life, global consequences

These human-generated influences on the planetary level are there-fore having an effect upon what we do on a daily basis, because they translate into localized problems of flooding and drought, problems with soil erosion (see also National Research Council (NRC) 2006) and depletion, and associated problems with population demands from basic health, shelter and well-being needs, through to the larger-scale issues of energy and food security.

These observations are not reserved to scientific commentators within the corporate world, which could be accused of contributing most to the systemic collapse through unsustainable business practice, there is an awakening of the consequences of global ecological collapse. Lloyds of London (2010) reported that the idea of business as usual is no longer a feasible way to respond to the set of global ecological challenges. In their annual analysis of risks to business, the Lloyds Group (ibid.) specifically identified water, food, energy and population as themes that have to be tackled to be attended to over the next 50 years. They comment:

Water

Only 3 per cent of the world's water is fresh and therefore suitable to sustain human life. As our populations continue to become participants in the global economy, one of the first resources that will peak, where demand outstrips supply, will be water. The combined challenge of urbanization and climate change will increase the strain on water resources, we have to learn to reduce our water useage and manage our water much more effectively.

Food

It is estimated that there will be a further 70–100 per cent increase in food production required to feed an expected population of 9.1 billion people by 2030. Recent poor growing conditions and mass parasitic events in 2008 aligned to prompt a food crisis in the Southern world. Between 2006 and 2008, the average world prices for rice rose by 217 per cent, wheat rose by 136 per cent, corn rose by 125 per cent and soya beans rose by 107 per cent. The price rises meant people could not afford to buy their basic foodstuffs. The result was food riots and civil disorder on an unprecedented scale across many cities of the South (Chomsky 2006).

Energy

The demand for energy across the planet is expected to rise in keeping with the rise in population. This comes at a time when the supply of recoverable gas is expected to last until 2030 at the latest. In a similar way that we have seen with water and food, the greater number of people participating in a global economy focused upon growth will substantially increase the supply shortfall. Added to this is the recognition that fossil fuels contribute to climate change, this challenges fossil fuels' likelihood of being a sustainable source of energy in the future if we are to ensure that we reduce carbon emissions.

Population

For the first time in human history, more people live in urban environments than in rural. Since 1987, China has witnessed 400 million new urbanites through economic modernization, and it expects a further 300 million people to move from the country to the city from 2005 to 2020. To accommodate this vast number of new city dwellers, a building programme of immense proportion has started, creating 400 new cities by 2020. There are over 220 cities in China with populations of more than one million, and eight mega-cities with more than ten million residents. There are only 35 such cities in Europe.

What these continually evolving environmental changes represent is uncharted territory for the human race. If the data are correct, we will all be facing significant changes to our physical environment as a result of climate change (Brown 2002, 2003). As we witness a whole new level of communal relationships as our cities grow ever bigger, a practical challenge will correspondingly grow for the already stretched governance, logistical and management services that operate across our societies. This has become a regular expression of concern from commentators across civic, economic and environmental communities, but it speaks to the very poorest in our world most profoundly, as they are the people who are going to bear the brunt of the effects earliest because they will be unable to buy their way out of trouble. Consequently, it is galvanizing international attention. Recognizing the particular demands that climate change will have upon energy and food security, the Heads of Government of the Commonwealth concluded in their joint declaration: 'with fossil fuels being a finite resource and the urgent threat of climate change, ensuring safe, reliable and affordable energy for the people ... was a fundamental challenge.' And for food security they expressed their

... deep concern about the threats that climate change, lack of access to fresh water resources, dumping of toxic waste and volatile commodity and energy prices pose to world food security (they called for) increased investment in sustainable agriculture, rural development, and natural resource management, including innovative practices, and stressed the importance of a coherent, multi-dimensional approach to sustainable agricultural development and food security.

(pp. 42–43)

System of systems – interconnectivity

These examples illustrate a greater insight, one that has arrived as a result of converging scientific fields over the last few decades; namely that our earth systems can be thought of as a single, interconnected, self-regulating entity, a notion that was originally formed by the scientist James Lovelock in his Gaia theory. His recent work (2006/2009) gives stark warnings of the dangers we face as a result of temperature rise, and how our efforts need to be far more radical than we have previously imagined. Lovelock and many of the community who study the complex issue of climate change are beginning to converge on a rise of 5°C globally higher than now as a plateau point. Once it gets to this point, the system self-regulates again at a much hotter norm, but the carrying capacity of the planet for human beings becomes considerably less than it is today. Lovelock estimates no more than one billion people will survive on the planet by the end of the twenty-first century. It will be too hot for things to grow and people will starve, because our geopolitical systems will not move fast enough to attend to the challenges: it is a bleak picture.

The concern has implications for action on all levels, it might begin at the macro – the global level – but returns to the micro – the neighbourhood and what we might do ourselves – it is therefore of universal importance. The scale, scope and stakes are all starting to make some sense and efforts are emerging at all levels of our systems to focus attention and ensure some form of meaningful response.

What to do?

We know the worst case scenario, and we know that we have to extend our capability to live with the change that will come. What we do becomes a vital consideration (Kellstedt *et al.* 2008). Brand suggests three broad strategic responses to climate change: mitigation, adaptation and amelioration.

1   *Mitigation*: Cut back greenhouse gas emissions.
2   *Adaptation*: Manage the unavoidable, move coastal population to higher places, develop drought tolerant agriculture, prepare for mass migration of climate refugees, localize resource warfare where people fight for their survival.
3   *Amelioration*: Adjust the natural circumstances through large-scale geo-engineering.

(Brand 2009: 13)

So what does all of this mean? It suggests that those of us alive on the planet today will play a huge role in the next exploration of our species history. What we do, how we intervene, how we think about the agenda all converge around a question of survival and a redefinition of progress and development. Whereas past generations have been the victims of circumstance, we are now largely authors of our own destiny. While civilization is at risk, it is also the case that a particular form of civilization is the problem. We are the main cause of many of the positive feedback loops on the planet as a consequence of how we have chosen to live and do business. The conflict lies in ways of thinking and acting, particularly where economics meets with planetary well-being. As biologist Tim Flannery[3] says: 'The metabolism of our economy is now on a collision course with the metabolism of our planet.'

The focus to establish sustainable conditions for human existence on the earth has therefore become an international concern, and its rise on the international agenda carries with it the tension that is present between contemporary economy and earth.

One manifestation of this concern is the term 'sustainable development' first adopted by the United Nations in the Brundtland Commission (United Nations 1987) that defined sustainable development as a set of conditions that satisfy 'the needs of the present without compromising the ability of future generations to meet their own needs'. It was an extremely important report, which was mostly ignored. There are perhaps numerous reasons why sustainable development has for more than a quarter of a century failed to ignite the public imagination. Possibly because people are not all that interested in bureaucratic responses to problems, they like to see practical example that can inspire and guide, rather than regulatory frameworks and diktat. Fundamentally, the report imagined that the practice of sustainable development would combine concern for the carrying capacity of natural systems with the social challenges facing humanity, through which we would develop into a new-found security of environment, community and economy. It seems to have been fabricated upon the modern agenda, that business can continue as usual but there might be a slight speed bump ahead.

The connection between natural and economic growth has been dealt with administratively rather than, for example, socially, scientifically or culturally. Our divisions continue to exist between these variables and show little sign of abating. This point about administration matters, as it indicates the direction of travel of many of the debates that led up to, and have subsequently followed on from, the many conferences and meetings that the term has spawned. To achieve the intention of meeting current and future needs without compromise, the concept of sustainable development was divided into three critical components: environmental sustainability, economic sustainability and sociopolitical sustainability. Each component of the sustainable development jigsaw was then pursued with restorative intent, with the aim being that its agents would participate in restorative action: it has sometimes integrated and embedded as a way of thinking acting and being, it frequently gets bolted on the end of policies and practices and consequently becomes an isolated, rather than an integrated, concern.

Despite its widespread use as a terminology to describe efforts to ensure responsible forms of growth, the sustainable development concept remains. It is still the case that, despite international efforts, the carbon emissions continue to rise, and we are still on a trajectory which makes the 5°C rise look increasingly likely by end-century (Allison 2009: 11) (and there are those who argue that positive feedback will accelerate the likelihood of reaching these numbers much sooner). While recognizing the good intentions, Lovelock (2006, 2009) characteristically challenged the premise of sustainable development on a number of fronts, but his central argument suggested that its weakness as an idea lies in the fact that sustainable development 'represents the continuous effort to balance and integrate three pillars of social well-being, economic prosperity and environmental protection for the benefit of present and future generations'. Many consider this noble policy morally superior to the laissez-faire of business as usual. Unfortunately for us, these wholly different approaches – one the expression of international decency, the other of unfeeling market forces – have the same outcome: the probability of disastrous global change. The error they share is the belief that further development is possible and that Earth will continue, more or less as now, for at least the first half of this century. Two hundred years ago, when change was slow or non-existent, we might have had time to establish sustainable development, or even have continued for a while with business as usual, but now is much too late; the damage has already been done (Lovelock 2006: 3–4).

Lovelock's argument is that it is much too late for sustainable development, he makes a compelling case for what he calls sustainable retreat (ibid.: 8), challenging the conventional wisdom is a first order of action. We need to confront the practical realities of the evidence that we have now gathered on climate change, and act according to these data, not the 'persistence of incomplete world-views'.

Given this situation as a worst-case scenario, what might our best-case scenario look like? Brand (2009) concludes that we will not stop climate change, but we can work towards stopping worse climate change, or very much worse climate change. To do that we have to look at carbon reduction, and to get there we have to explore and implement energy solutions which can provide the power we need to run our civilization or, alternatively, we have to look at a new way of running civilization that does not require as much power (Hopkins 2008). Technically we are capable of solving the power problem; politically it is a much bigger task. This seemingly translates much further, however, into the day-to-day things people do, which in turn have a bearing on the possibility of new ways of living. Mitigation, adaptation and amelioration are not just the macro-economic actions of government, they are the practical stuff of our individual lives, they are our civilization, our cultures, our habits of mind and deed, and they are embedded in our ways of educating.

Just as sustainable development is wedded to an industrial economic growth model, modern education and schooling are conceived upon those incomplete world-views that have led to the technical certainties of the performance culture. Over a number of years, some of my work has examined how this approach to education contributes to, rather than resolves, many of the problems in our schools (see Clarke 2005). Education is wedded to the same industrial-economic model, measured through GNP, and suffers the same fundamental, structural and hierar-chically conceived problems. It perpetuates a system through which we create citizens as consumers, reliant upon continuous economic and industrial growth and personal wealth. Yet look around and we can see widespread evidence that this, the old order, is crumbling and its finan-cial system is in tatters (Soros 2008). It is as if we are stuck with only one way forward and despite its failings we dare not consider an alterna-tive for fear that things will get worse, but how much worse do we want them to get? We do not warm to the idea that things are only going to get worse, one reason why connecting to the climate change challenge is so difficult; our general outlook as a species tends towards a concern for ourselves, we need to imagine a future beyond the existing order of things (Carson 1962) that can be translated into a vision of human development, or perhaps we should describe it as human progress that steps from under the current impasse.

Education of the ecological attitude?

This is all part of the difficult territory of educational change and real moral purpose – where we might begin to fashion a new set of measures, where the effort is focused upon a need to transform the whole idea of education as a preparation of our communities for sustainable living (see Alexander *et al.* 1977, Barth *et al.* 2007), it does not necessarily come in the form of 'sustainable development' (Jickling 1992). It comes instead through our communities becoming capable of functioning effectively as a result of a composite of sustainable practices; these are based around relationships, places, interests and actions where an appreciation and value of the ecological is the frame through which all other aspects of human activity are then designed and promoted, with science and technology playing a critical role in combining the urban with the rural. If we consider the role of education in this way, we can explore it on the basis of prosperity to enhance economic, cultural, personal and societal terms, through the lens of how we relate to our planet and each other. This formulation of response is clearly different from that which has been advanced by advocates of sustainable development, and embeds the notion of sustainability within an ecological context as a continually developing, emergent ambition. In fact, the notion of development as we currently conceive it is simply not part of the idea of Ecological Sustainability. Instead, we might think of development in this new way as something we achieve when we establish suitable conditions to live sustainably while maintaining the diversity of life as the basis of development or productivity so, for example, we can begin to establish some new ways to measure the impact of our efforts:

- Society must have the capability and resilience to solve and preferably prevent its major problems in a timely fashion.
- Society's aggregate use of resources and land must be ultra-frugal.
- Material flows into and out of society must not systematically increase.
- The human population must be sustainable.
- Actions must be timely and at an adequate scale.

To establish these items, people need to be in a position to be informed enough to be able to solve and prevent major problems in a timely fashion, so they may be characterized through qualities such as:

- an elimination of corruption and a commitment to honest practice;
- participatory action;
- diverse, divergent and constant experimentation;
- inclusive, caring, cohesive, tolerant communities;
- critical skills of analysis and reflection;
- creative and skilled processes of socialization;
- anticipatory abilities, future scoping and pattern understanding;
- conservation of valuable aspects of present and past;
- commitment to the achievement of the social good and collective well-being;
- ability to give adequate time to civic activity and community;
- adequate resource and equipment to ensure that the civic infrastructure, knowledge and skills are maintained and enhanced;
- a political system(s) which can achieve these objectives.

These qualities represent a major cultural undertaking, but they are qualities that are already present and advanced in many of our existing school environments, they form what is often described as an ethos. This ethos is simply a way of thinking, acting and being which defines the way we go about our daily lives in our learning communities, it is *an attitude*. What is different, and will need further consideration, is a deliberate focus upon ecological reasoning, and it is this, as Macy and Young Brown (2008) argue, that can be understood as the essential adventure for our time – a shift from the Industrial Growth Society to a life-sustaining civilization. What is interesting is that it is already happening, not because anyone planned it, but because circumstances have forced people to reappraise how they live due to changes in the economic circumstances of their lives.

> *For example:* Detroit was once the mainstay of the US motor car industry. Today it has lost over 50 per cent of its citizens as the industrial legacy collapsed and people left for work elsewhere. But not all the people left. As old structures came down people in the city began to redefine their communities, the estimated 25–30 per cent of the vacant lots across the city represented an opportunity for a growing urban agriculture movement to move in and re-model and reclaim the land in Detroit to grow food. There are over 1,200 community, school and family gardens, and several

city centre farms have been established. One of the largest urban farms is called D-Town Farm. It was founded by the Detroit Black Community Food Security Network, a coalition of individuals and organizations which combined to establish food security in the largely black community. D-Town Farm is described by the chairman, Malik Yakini, as a two-acre site inside of a city park, it is based on a ten-year licence agreement to establish a model organic farm and demonstrate how underutilized land can be put to productive use to create greater access to fresh produce and to mobilize people to work on their own behalf. The network supports people in training and learning so that the community has adequate amounts of quality food that is easily accessible and food secure. Lack of access to quality food has enormous health implications, including diabetes, obesity, and high blood pressure; all of which can be controlled by diet. The collapse of the inner city service sector (supermarkets) meant that people had no choice but to act to ensure that they were supporting themselves and facilitating control and ownership of their own land, managed by themselves, and modelling the revenue and social and political and economic dynamics that were appropriate to the people in the local community. Their efforts are being seen as acts of self-determination and self-empowerment to enrich themselves, not others, and in growing food and developing the urban agriculture movement they are enabling the people to see how they can work on their own behalf, and for their own benefit; this in turn enables people to hold politicians to account and mobilize to ensure that their relationship with their political officials is on a new basis of respect and mutual understanding.

This is a re-evaluation of how people can live together in urban spaces on a grand scale, it embeds the rural ethic into the urban space and it is happening in the most advanced industrialized country of the world. The Detroit network demonstrates a characteristic revision of public space in a manner that is happening all over the world, North and South, where people are recognizing the power that can be mobilized through direct action arising through the awakening of a new economic and environmental consciousness of urban and rural convergence. Macy and Young Brown (2008) write about this saying:

> People are recognizing that our needs cannot be met without destroying our world, We have the technical knowledge, the communication tools, and material resources to grow enough food,

ensure clean air and water, and meet rational energy needs. Future generations, if there is a livable world for them, will look back at the epochal transition we are making to a life-sustaining society … And it is gaining momentum through the actions of countless individuals and groups around the world. To see this as the larger context of our lives clears our vision and summons our courage.

A climate of change

Without saying as much, the growers of downtown Detroit, along with the academics and scientists such as Joanna Macy, Molly Young Brown and Jim Lovelock, are arguing for a revolution of our urban mind, which will lead to change in behaviour with relative amounts of belief that this will in fact make a difference. They are saying that we need to establish a suitable human response that is in keeping with the environmental disequilibrium we are witnessing, and this response has to take precedence over all other demands, including economic demands, if we have a chance of surviving the century relatively intact as a species.

In such complex and challenging circumstances, where pressures are going to increase at the international level for greater cooperation and connectivity, any economy that is governed by the singular desire for profit and industrially driven growth, rather than collective planning for human need, is going to be increasingly unsustainable. The degree of connectedness that is now available through social networking technologies means that we are on the move towards a whole new version of human civilization. People can connect both globally and locally in ways that were almost inconceivable less than a decade ago. As we go towards that new civilization, and our attention is taken up with responding to the huge changes that are going to come as a result of climate change, we will ourselves change, in our lifestyles and our communities. We are becoming increasingly urban, our villages are emptying out and, interestingly, as we become more urbanized we are more aware of the natural systems upon which we depend, and we are showing signs through wilderness protection schemes, through pollution control and through the normalizing of the green agenda into our urban space requirements. This is helping to shape a new way of looking at our relationship with the world.

Even if we are not just yet at the endgame of the old order, we are indeed in a significant period of existential and physical disequilibrium within our taken-for-granted systems of social and economic organization. As Havel's quote at the start of this Exploration emphasizes, as one set of circumstances begins to fragment, a new set of circumstances begins to rise; such is the way of change. The questions we might begin to consider are obviously influenced by the bigger context, but in considering such global shifts we might ask what and how those circumstances look like in the micro, community context within which our schools function, and how well will they be able to facilitate and nurture the conditions for ecological sustainability – or will there be a need for a more guided and structured set of sustainable community ideas?

What is also clear is an underlying assumption that we will find the appropriate mode of instruction to facilitate the move from one way of living to a whole new level of living. This signals a radical overhaul of how we modify the destructive tendencies of capitalist consumer society. As Tim Jackson from the New Economics Foundation observes, we need new models of learning that render the existing ways of seeing our complex reality as obsolete (Jackson 2009), primarily because the existing industrial models have generated the conditions that have created the global ecological crisis in the first place (Soros 2008).

The connection between the natural story and the human story is therefore one of awareness, down to past, present and future measures of our action, and in particular the balance between environmental permanence and what we call 'development' or 'growth'. Instead of simply measuring economic output, an emphasis on ecological sustainability raises the bar for communities to redefine their presence on the earth. If we recognize our role as contributors to the ecological disaster we can now witness around the planet, then we might assume our defining questions become questions of the dynamics of relationships: How do the human and natural narratives co-exist? Are they in crisis? Do we currently have the wisdom to make appropriate judgments to live and flourish within an ever-changing, emergent reality?

As we have indicated, scientific evidence over the past decade is increasingly converging on the view that climate change is evident across the planet, yet on its own, we know, people do not respond to such data. This response is, in itself, an indicator that our relationship with the earth is far from harmonious and at a sufficiently significant state of disequilibrium to consider how we might change track. It was the Nobel laureate Ilya Prigogine who said, as long as a system is stable, or at an equilibrium, you can't change it, but as it moves toward disequilibrium and falls into chaos then the slightest bit of coherent energy can bring it into a new structure. It would appear that we are now operating within such a time. With that chaos comes great opportunity for radical transformation.

Summary

This Exploration has suggested that there are a number of contributory factors which are connected through changing climate: these are water – too much, too little or too polluted; food and food security being threatened by climate changes; energy and the reliability and maintenance of energy sources as demands get ever more excessive; and population growth and the inevitable demands a growing population places upon resources.

Sketching out the underlying themes that form the foundations of the story of our unsustainable way of living is not difficult; the evidence is all around us. However, as we become more aware of the intricate connections between natural systems and our human systems, we also begin to see the possibility of new ways to proceed; this is the fabric of just such a design for sustainable living.

In the next Exploration, I will examine the basis of the response within the educational sector, to the need for educational engagement with the challenges posed by our unsustainable civilization.

Notes

1 Greenhouse gas is a collective term for those gases which reduce the loss of heat from the earth's atmosphere, and thus contribute to global warming and climate change.
2 GWP – a measure of a greenhouse gas's ability to absorb heat and warm the atmosphere over a given time period.
3 Australian scientist Tim Flannery told Australian Broadcasting Corporation that a report by the UN Intergovernmental Panel on Climate Change (IPCC) contains new data showing that the level of climate-changing gases in the atmosphere has already reached critical levels. Flannery is not a member of the IPCC, but said he based his comments on a thorough review of the technical data included in the panel's three working group reports published earlier in 2007. The IPCC released its final report synthesizing the data in November 2007. Flannery (2007) went on to say: 'What the report establishes is that the amount of greenhouse gas in the atmosphere is already above the threshold that can potentially cause dangerous climate change. We are already at great risk of dangerous climate change, that's what these figures say. It's not next year or next decade, it's now.'

Exploration Two
Is education fit for purpose if the purpose is sustainable living?

We're the first generation with tools to understand changes in the Earth's system caused by human activity, and the last with the opportunity to influence the course of many of the changes now rapidly under way.
Vitousek et al. *1997*

What was outlined in the first Exploration was a narrative of both anticipated and actual change, as evidenced through change already present in the form of pressures upon the carrying capacity of the planet in essential areas that are vital for life, and change that is predicted – both pose a threat to human civilization. It is worth noting that we did not go about deliberately creating these disturbing ecological conditions. They came about because of the systemic consequences of human activity. We have learned to live in a particular way, it just so happens to be a particularly unsustainable way. The sum of our actions has given rise to their existence. The character of this change is therefore important. As human industrial activity has grown, the overlayering of our activities has begun to establish toxic conditions. As we grow more aware of these conditions, our analysis of the complexity of the problem deepens. Exactly how we respond begins to be an important issue in itself. What we do, ought to be the consequence of what we know. What we know is that our approach to urban industrial life must change, and this in turn raises the question of how to facilitate such change.

In the first part of this Exploration, I want to focus on the way international action has prompted strategic responses. I will then suggest why it has failed so far to provide a way forward at the system level. My argument is that it has not succeeded because of one really simple but immensely important part of the transformational narrative that needs to emerge if the established industrial world is to evolve radically. It is best summed up as a shift of mind, 'metanoia', the Greek word for conversion, described as a 'fundamental transformation of mind'. The word captures the process by which concepts become reorganized. It is one result of an attentive mind, focused upon a discipline, where reality is considered, challenged and changed as a result of a serious shift that takes us out of ourselves and considers our universal presence, and formulates a new way of thinking that is informed by nature, an eco-centric vision of reality. The metanoia *is the shift* from ego to eco. It implies much more than a simple realignment of organizational structures – it is a fundamental shift of the meaning of progress enshrined, as it were, within an ecological and not an industrial paradigm. This is the context of the ecological metanoia, and without such a shift we will remain locked to a formulaic and instrumental design for reform that will ultimately not provide the contextual conditions for people to be able to make the required changes. The transformation, from ego to eco is an important component because, without it, we remain on a course of living which exploits, extracts and consumes with insufficient attention to the dependencies we have to the planet (Webster and Johnson 2009). Once we get the point that we are a part of the planet, and not apart from the planet, all the rest of the story comes together and our manufacturing, our economics, our culture begin to align themselves in a slightly different, but much more life-sustaining, manner – we need to become Naturally Smart.

Whereas at present the ecological challenge is often defined technically in the form of climate measurements and the associated reduction activities, where we can gather the data, measure the temperature rise, witness the ice-melt, the desertification and deforestation increase by the acre (see for example IPCC 2004), we know that it will be resolved not through technologies and measurement alone, it will be resolved through a change in our cultures, through our social, economic, political, creative and spiritual sensibilities.

Such is the challenge, to evolve new ways of educating people to think and act in response to the problem, to establish activities that in themselves may seem rather mundane, but which facilitate change in human behaviour and move our cultures towards an evolved consciousness[1] (see Figure 1). The intention, then, is to urgently generate structural change throughout society, but to do so particularly within the organizational frameworks of the establishment (for example through schools), as they are the main carriers of the existing dysfunction. As people witness their ecological practices change, they provide our cultures with templates for action. As we adopt the new

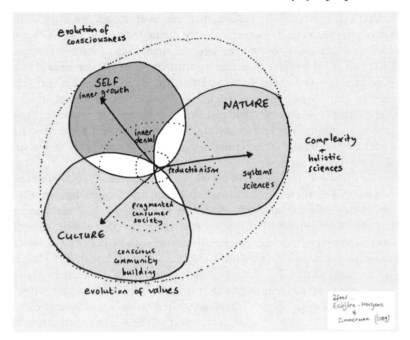

Figure 1 From ego to eco.

story, we will formulate a new set of values – ecologically aligned – and these begin to replace the existing industrial story with something new.

The combined changes to culture, self and relationship with natural systems represent the basis of the changes to which I am referring throughout this book. While these ideas are not new (see Esbjorn-Hargens and Zimmerman 2009), the location of the ideas within a post-modern period of cultural transition (characterized by a desired move from egocentric, reductivist and fragmented reality) serves as a guide to our understanding. Through conscious effort to build community, integrate knowledge systems and deepen an understanding of self, we may evolve on three complementary planes – towards more ecologically sustainable human consciousness, embedded values within our societies and holistic sciences in our knowledge base.

Much of this process is intuitive rather than predetermined (see Atkinson and Claxton 2000), our narratives are fluid, emergent and layered and will themselves facilitate new metaphors which will in turn help us to see a different set of social conditions in process (Hundertwasser 2006). It is therefore not to be seen as a predetermined direction of travel, but if we are to believe that our institutions, structures and systems have an effect upon the way we define reality, then we put some trust in their ability to change and, in changing, to have a systemic effect upon the social, economic, spiritual and cultural narratives. These evolving narratives help us to redefine the relationship between the human and the natural; we redefine our coexistence with nature (see Benus 2008 for examples). It reveals the need for new understanding and new cultural metaphors through which a different form of social order can be established and ritualized, and our schools are places where such work can take place.

This is not wishful or pie-in-the-sky thinking, because a problem that has bedevilled the environmental movement for decades has been the association of a certain form of lifestyle that drops out of mainstream culture. While some of the actions of these people provide us with useful examples, there are fundamental problems with the environmental movement's tendency to drop-out rather than take-on and change mainstream society. It is no longer an 'us and them' problem. For one thing, there are too many of us to run to the hills, the idea therefore of self-sufficiency, a phrase often associated with environmental life choices, is of limited value in the context of the urban mega-cities, we are fundamentally a social and interdependent species as demonstrated through our urban world. This connection to a global series of events, from whatever place we might find ourselves on the planet, is perhaps in itself a very important part of the message of change to which we have to acclimatize (Aune 2009). Looking at the problem through the urban lens therefore raises the prospect of seeing the human system as a colonial question: how to provide mass populations with models and templates to colonize sustainably on a global scale. We are seeking practical and pragmatic responses to the presenting evidence of changing global circumstances, and by facing it as a systemic problem, and thinking about it as a societal response as well as a personal response, we begin to formulate new insights into how we might make progress. What is interesting, however, is that this is exactly what is happening worldwide. The challenge is how to formulate the stories.

From policy to practice?

One set of powerful stories that seeks to connect sustainability and education are conceived at policy level, and are concerned with the structure and function of our institutions. They represent a persistent political belief in the architecture of organization as a source of change, and the effective management of systems as a solution to the practicalities of all our daily lives. The concern is to get the right policies in place, which in turn will then provide the operational clarity for people to adopt the appropriate responses to systemic sustainability problems (Binney and Williams 1995). This approach is a characteristic of governance and management systems across industrialized democratic human systems around the world.

The concept of sustainable development was established by the World Commission on Environment and Development in the Stockholm Declaration of 1972. In the same year, the UN Conference on Environment and Development (UNCED) produced a working document known as Agenda 21 that set the scene for sustainable development but failed to make the critical connection to education (Agenda 21). It was a decade later, in 2002, when the UN Earth Summit on Sustainable Development was held in Johannesburg, that a direct link between education, learning and sustainability was formed. However, it was also extended to a range of issues such as economic and social development, health, effective governance, trade and environment (UNESCO 2002).

The incorporation of sustainability thinking into higher education was emphasized by the UN's Decade of Education for Sustainable Development (2005–2014) (UNESCO 2002). The central themes assigned to this decade of action reflect the major issues outlined in Agenda 21, together with the action plans of the subsequent UN conferences concerning sustainable development focusing on 'promoting education, public awareness and training'. It identified three programme areas for education and learning:

1   Reorienting education to sustainable development.
2   Increasing public awareness.
3   Promoting training.[2]

Clearly, the international agreements form a policy framework through which practice would be encouraged, but the precise methods were still unfolding from these formative announcements.

Education for sustainable development is best understood as a lifelong capacity building process which enhances the personal, community, regional and national capacity to respond to the need for a sustainable world. With its focus upon social, economic and environmental issues that threaten the sustainability of the planet (Scott and Gough 2003: 19), its ambition is inevitably broad. It includes an understanding of personal, ecological, cultural and historical values, the values of present and possible future societies, and the values of cultures around the world as a central part of educating for a sustainable future.

Part of the capacity-building capability of education for sustainable development lies in social justice and inclusion (Tilbury 2011). Social justice includes respect for the traditions and religions of other cultures and societies – as well as ensuring intergenerational social justice through ecological sustainability and resource conservation. Preserving and conserving the physical planetary resource base provides disadvantaged communities with a legal right to claim sanctuary against multinational exploitation of land and mineral resources and, in theory at least, this prevents people from living long term in disadvantaged circumstances and can enhance their chances of having a better life (McKeown 2002: 18).

Education for sustainable development is presented as an inclusive approach, it brings together all the learning that a person does throughout life, in both formal and informal settings. Because it is a lifelong process, it has encouraged collaboration between formal, non-formal and informal educational sectors to accomplish local sustainability goals.

Education for sustainable development is represented through four pillars (Scott and Gaugh 2003):

1   Learning to know.
2   Learning to do.
3   Learning to live together.
4   Learning to be.

Because education for sustainable development is concerned with the natural environment, it is to be understood as an emergent and evolving concept rather than a set of fixed or predetermined views. As education for sustainable development is adopted, it provides individuals and their organizations with a way of understanding both global and local issues in a coherent context. It encourages all members of the organization to adopt forecasting as a way of visualizing possible futures based on a range of different scenarios, in this way it attempts to overcome dogmatic and deterministic approaches to change. In contrast to traditional transmission-oriented education, education for sustainable development focuses on developing competences. It adopts a range of pedagogic approaches, encouraging project-based learning, multidisciplinary case studies, role playing, task-based learning and cross-disciplinary problem-solving. The emphasis here is that to succeed in making education for sustainable development effective, learners must be able to apply their knowledge within a practical multi-disciplinary and interdisciplinary context.

A further dimension of education for sustainable development that is of particular importance for school settings is the emphasis on establishing a community of learners. Education for sustainable development encourages teachers, students and other stakeholders to combine their focus to ensure that different members of the learning community undertake different roles.

> *For example:* the student may take an active role in the learning process and collaborate with others in the classroom, laboratory and in the field. Members of staff and other stakeholders might act as mentors, supervisors and guides to assist the students in discovering, applying and understanding information, technical and scientific knowledge, and different kinds of skills. In this way the learning experience becomes more dynamic and iterative (generating new cross-disciplinary knowledge) than it would in traditional subject-governed courses.

Learning about sustainable development is therefore best described as a joint search among individuals and organizations for knowledge and competencies that enable them to deal with dilemmas in complex social settings (Holmberg and Samuelsson 2006: 17). The emphasis upon learning how to tackle complex problems when working with experts from different disciplinary domains directs the curricula activity towards the practical. The point is to help people build a personal and social capability so that, as lifelong learners, they are able to manage the tensions that arise between their own needs and those of others.

What is the impact?

The policy ambitions of education for sustainable development have had varying degrees of impact and effect across nations.

In some places, such as Finland, Norway, Sweden and Denmark, education for sustainable development has always been a significant element of the educational process and their approach has pioneered innovative thinking on the benefits of outdoor learning for children.

One example of the Scandinavian design of education for sustainable development comes in the Forest School which originated in Sweden in the 1950s, has developed extensively throughout other Scandinavian Countries, and is starting to gain a foothold elsewhere. The Forest Schools concept became a substantive feature of Danish education for pre-school children (under seven years) in the 1980s and stemmed from their småbørnspædagogik or Early Years Education and, by the mid-1990s, was being visited by people from many other European countries as an example of an educational approach that provided significant support for child development.

Studies carried out in Sweden, and subsequently Japan (Grahn *et al.* 1997, Shimizu *et al.* 2002) on forest school and outdoor learning found in both cases that children attending forest school kindergartens in the countryside environment are far happier than children in kindergartens located in the urban environment. The studies both concluded that children in the forest school are more balanced with greater socially capability, they have fewer days off sick. The results also showed the children attending the forest school to be markedly better at concentrating than the city Kindergarten children. It appeared that the principle reasons identified were due to the greater range of opportunities available for play in nature – children played for longer, with less adult and fellow student interruption, compared to the children in the city kindergarten. The study observed that when children in the city kindergarten were interrupted, they became irritable, their stress levels rose significantly, and their ability to concentrate fell. When they could not concentrate there was a clear tendency to selfish, aggressive and inconsiderate behaviour. The forest school children were much more considerate of each other. Children attending forest school kindergartens were reported to be arriving at mainstream school with stronger social skills, greater ability to work in groups, and holding high self-esteem and confidence in their own capabilities. All these attributes provide an effective foundation that raises academic achievement.

Elsewhere, the approach adopted to education for sustainable living has been directed through municipal and environmental programmes of government, rather than directly through educational projects.

For example, in Australia, the physical consequences of climate change are already well understood and recognized across the community, and this practical knowledge has translated into school curricula and building design with every school being required to address measures for securing shade and safety awareness of excessive sunshine – but it is interesting to note that the primary policy document which defined the agenda for education for sustainable development came not from the government education department, but instead from the Department of Environment, Water, Heritage and the Arts.[3]

Similarly in China, an environmental rather than educational route to sustainable education has been adopted, but this has been translated into regional and localized activity and seems to be taking effect through structural and technical reforms, which in turn are leading to pedagogical change. The Green Schools initiative from the Ministry of Education of China is funded by the State through the Environmental Protection Administration. China's Green Schools programme, which started in 1996, was influenced by the European 'Eco-schools' Programmes. Since 2000, it has been run by the Centre for Environmental Education and Communications through a network of local resource centres. The programme includes a focus upon whole-school environmental management and protection initiatives, environmental education curriculum and supporting professional development, and a greening of school grounds. To receive the prestigious award of being called a Green School, a series of steps have to be undertaken, which grow increasingly more demanding for the school community to achieve, attending to issues such as:

- ways to ensure site and ecosystem protection:
    - through the identification and monitoring of indigenous flora and fauna and the use of native landscaping;
    - avoiding materials that might cause harm to the environment;
    - preserving and restoring natural features;
- preservation and improvement of the environment:
    - through erosion and sediment control;
    - through the creation or restoration of ponds and streams and through the simple introduction of straw bales and other basic materials to establish terraces and deep growing beds;
- reduction of unwanted heat in buildings:
    - by creating green roofs and ensuring reflective and light-building colours;
- energy conservation:
    - through management of the daily use of energy across a school;
    - through procurement of suitable low-energy solutions to basic lighting, and the design and retrofit to ensure greater use of direct and indirect natural light sources.

Awards are categorized through a staged development process, starting at municipal, provincial and then national levels. The range of strategies and projects adopted in response to the Green Schools challenge are impressive.

For example, one school set up a project to reduce the heat emitted from the school building. It is widely recognized that dark buildings can absorb heat, which has a cumulative effect upon a local setting, can be harmful to wildlife and have an adverse effect on biodiverse habitats. The students worked together to establish counter-measures to the negative effects of the building which involved adopting a green roof, planting trees and flowers, using light colours on walls and reflective materials to reduce heat absorption. The result of this work then led them to look into the cooling and efficiency possibilities of water management. Throughout school they started to redesign and retrofit the school landscape in such a way as to draw public attention to more efficient uses and storage of water. This included reduction in water use, growing hardy, native plants, using drip irrigation systems instead of sprinkler systems, capturing and recycling water, and designing new ways of holding water for non-potable uses. In every level of the work the students were engaged in the design and data collection which now serves as a baseline for the future activity of the school.

Elsewhere, an economic course of action is being adopted. In April 2011, the US Department of Education announced the creation of the Green Ribbon Schools programme, which will recognize schools that have made efforts to green their curricula, buildings, school grounds and overall building operations. The Green Ribbon School awards will be given to schools that best exemplify America's transition to a sustainable economy, from graduating environmentally literate students, to effectively managing their carbon footprint. The programme is designed to encourage school systems to take a comprehensive approach to becoming a green school by cutting expenses through energy efficiency and green building measures, while at the same time using these sustainable school improvements as part of their efforts to educate students about science, technology and the environment.

The US Department of Energy estimates that smarter energy management in schools, which spent $6–$8 billion on energy in 2000, could reduce energy consumption by as much as 25 per cent and cut school energy costs nationally by more than $1 billion annually. However, the social and civic benefits of adopting 'green' measures are also identified, and so hitting a 'triple bottom line' of economy, society and environment, very much in keeping with the basic tenets of sustainable development. Rick Fedrizzi, President, CEO and founding chair, of the US Green Building Council said in a press release: 'No other building type speaks more profoundly to the benefits of green building than the places where our children learn. Green schools reduce energy consumption, save money and foster healthier learning environments for our children.'

In the United Kingdom, there is a very mixed picture of impact at the individual school level but policy follows a similar trajectory to that of the broad schema of education for sustainable development. Scotland,

Wales and Northern Ireland have all established successful sustainable schools initiatives, functioning within policy frameworks but enabling schools to take considerable initiative themselves:

Two examples: In Merthyr Tydfil, South Wales, a school is working to establish a design for a transition of their High School grounds to a community farm. The Cyfarthfa Farm Transition project is a curriculum embedded programme which has four goals:

1   To lead to greater respect for the school environment.
2   To create a much more aesthetically pleasing learning environment.
3   To facilitate transition from lower to upper school.
4   To raise literacy standards.

In themselves these goals seem to bear little difference to existing school improvement projects. However, the difference perhaps begins to become clearer when we examine the focus of the initiative. The entire school 'farm' project is based outdoors, and focused around a series of planned changes to the existing school fields and landscape, which in turn will generate new curriculum opportunities for the students ranging from the management of growing sites such as allotment spaces, to the maintenance and management of systems to reduce energy use across school, to ensure the site remains attractive and inviting, and to managing the responses and ideas of fellow members of the school community. To reach this position, a thorough study was undertaken of the different aspects of the school landscape and these were then structured around a series of eight specific development zones, each having a particular set of environmental challenges or features which the team of teachers and students are responding to in their own planning and design projects. These range from the tarmac car park at the front of school, which is being redesigned to include a sensory garden entrance area, and a series of planters which will host fruit bushes, strawberries and apple trees, to a livestock area which is currently a derelict parcel of land where students will construct chicken sheds and care for chickens, a vegetable growing scheme which will include a micro-business project to establish a box scheme for old people who live close to the school site. The scheme provides scope for each zone to be featured within the existing curriculum with minor adaptation of syllabus, and a series of staff development sessions have taken place to raise awareness, to enable each staff member to identify potential ways of participating through existing teaching practices, and for a working group to explore the possible ways that the project can be developed as the different zones begin to function as eco-zones in the school farm.

A second example is Mayfield Primary School, North Ayrshire. The staff visited an established community growing scheme (Incredible Edible – see Exploration Four) and created a short film of their visit. This film served as a starting point with students and parents for an evening meeting to discuss how to develop the use of the school grounds to include an orchard and forest garden, a vegetable patch and a herb garden. The staff worked together to identify a curriculum structure where each year group would engage directly with one aspect of the landscape and undertake a substantial part of their learning through their outdoor experiences in that landscape. Themes included Jack and the Beanstalk (an early years growing project with peas and beans), a market garden project (where children grow and use the produce as a market stall to sell to parents as a business awareness project), a sustainable structures project (where children design and build greenhouses by re-using old plastic bottles, and design and build seating areas with straw bales and willow), flowers and colours project (where bee- and bug-friendly flowers were sown and the mini-beasts and insects were monitored), and a composting and waste project (where soil composition and management were explored). Within one school year the entire school has become embedded into a landscape which was previously looking rather sparse, and turned it into a lively and interactive ecological resource for the school, and in time there are plans to extend this into community allotments for parents and to be able to run an after-school growing project.

In England, education for sustainable development has had a difficult period of transition from one governmental agenda to another. The Labour government target for every school to be a 'Sustainable School' by 2020 was supported by an increasing array of centrally conceived supporting structures such as the 'doorways' to sustainability. Doorways are a somewhat strange metaphor to adopt for a sustainability theme, but the initiative provided schools with some thematic models through which a sustainable programme of instruction and action could be developed. Themes included:

Food and drink	to be a model supplier of healthy, local and sustainable food and drink;
Energy and water	to be a model of energy efficiency, renewable energy use and water management;
Travel and traffic	to be a model of sustainable travel;
Purchasing and waste	to be a model of waste minimization and sustainable procurement;

Buildings and grounds	to ensure buildings and grounds help stakeholders learn about the natural world and sustainable living;
Inclusion and participation	to be a model of social inclusion, enabling all members of society to participate;
Local well-being	to be a model of good corporate citizenship within our local area;
Global perspective	to be a model of good global citizenship.

These themes have enabled individual and sometimes clusters of schools to explore within a structure, a way into thinking sustainably about their activity. The important emphasis here is to establish practice which can be used to 'model', and therefore function as a demonstrator site not just for the school but as a leading voice within a community.

For example, in Stanley Primary School, the school has designed a curriculum to ensure coverage of each of the doorways and they adapted these guidelines to provide a model through:

Energy use

This includes 24 electricity-generating solar panels which were installed in October 2006. The school is committed to energy conservation with a special Green Team responsible for turning off lights and computers at break and lunch times.

Biodiversity

The school hosts a set of environmental gardens and ponds to provide outdoor learning opportunities for the pupils.

All infant classes have raised, wooden troughs outside the classroom where they plant vegetable seeds and plants and the children are responsible for their upkeep. They visit this 'living classroom' regularly and have lessons on different aspects of the natural growing systems. The school set up a bird-cam and the children used it to monitor a mother bird raising her 13 baby blue tits from eggs through to hungry baby birds. A group of parents meet every Friday morning to work together in the Living Classroom to maintain and develop the area.

Growing schemes

All junior classes are given the opportunity to work on the five allotment beds throughout the year and help to produce organically grown food which the school sells to parents and uses in the school kitchens. The environmental garden, with its flourishing native hedgerow, wild meadow area, willow tunnel and bird boxes is regularly used by different classes.

Recycling

The school has a recycling and tidy team and has developed extensive recycling facilities to include paper, cardboard, tins and cans, plastic bottles, clothing, food, tin foil and batteries. The Junior Tidy Team are responsible for collecting paper and plastic bottles from around the school and recycling them, along with composting organic waste from the staffroom and school kitchens. The infant children have a dedicated recycling school counsellor who is responsible for monitoring energy use and recycling. There is a box in every classroom for paper and cardboard which is recycled regularly by the children.

Outreach

As well as attending to the themes implied in the basic doorways, the school has evolved new projects to extend its environmental outreach. These include:

- a monthly Fairtrade stall run by pupils and parents;
- dedicated environmentally themed lessons in all year groups;
- water butts which are used to water the Environmental Garden and water-saving 'Hippos' in all flushing toilets;
- bike and scooter racks to encourage pupils to cycle or scoot to school;
- a staff cycle rack;
- the use of a 'green' purchasing policy where they aim to purchase as many environmentally friendly products as possible;
- an active Eco-parent group which helps to generate new ideas and support new initiatives;
- taking part in the Walk on Wednesdays initiative encouraging children to walk to school at least once a week.

Clearly the doorways approach stimulated action and engagement with schools, and there are plenty of similar examples that could be pointed towards. Subsequently, however, the coalition government has abandoned the national strategy in favour of the encouragement of more localized approaches, and there is concern that the systemic possibilities that were beginning to emerge have been set back as schools have to realign to new political priorities. The significance of this move did not go unnoticed, and many observers are keeping a close eye on what might happen next in the English system. What was particularly poignant was the removal of all of the archive material on sustainable schools from the government website. This resource had been created by schools and school networks and served as a central resource for other schools to review and adopt, and this is no longer readily available.

However, the fundamental question remains. Does this form of education for sustainable development ensure a sufficiently radical reappraisal of the function and purpose of schools to help people build a personal and social capability so that, as lifelong learners, they are able to manage the tensions that arise between their own needs, those of others and critically, the needs of the planet?

In the English setting this question remains unanswered. What is quite evident in England is the huge variation in practice in the way in which schools have responded to the conceptual and pedagogical shift; that education for sustainable development demands has not resulted as yet in any clear sign of culture change; and that education is not yet fit for purpose if the purpose is sustainable living. Scratch the surface and you will find that the rhetoric of sustainable education is far from the reality. Education for sustainable development is often a marginal issue left mainly to interested activists and practitioners to undertake work in their own schools and communities. They do so with good intention, but one cannot help but think that in many circumstances the efforts reflect lifestyle choices, rather than a substantive pedagogical and practical change of behaviour. More widely, there is very little evidence of systemic, focused leadership at the national level in response to the general concerns over systemic environmental collapse, our education systems remain predominantly designed and 'delivered' along the lines of business as usual, or perhaps '*crisis, what crisis?*'

What is too often demonstrated is neither an integrated approach, nor something being adopted systemically as the means by which we design and develop our universal educational effort. This is in part because of the organizational structure of schools, where subject dominance that is driven by examination and qualification routes overrides any interdisciplinary innovation. The default educational position remains firmly within the industrial mode of schooling. Fundamentally, the majority of schools are still a long way from adopting any substantive model of education for sustainability methodologies (Hungerford and Volk 1990), perhaps because of the lack of regulatory requirements for them to demonstrate such activity in their practice, and perhaps simply due to lack of awareness – but it is also a failure of systemic practice, modelled through an industrialized transmission-based mode of practice which perhaps can influence structures but rarely reforms the receiving culture. These structural concerns have led to Tilbury's (2011) recent expert review of the impact so far of the decade of education for sustainable development to conclude and re-emphasize that certain key processes underpin the education for sustainable development frameworks for it to be successful. These include:

- processes of collaboration and dialogue (including multi-stakeholder and intercultural dialogue);
- processes which engage the 'whole system';
- processes which innovate curriculum as well as teaching and learning experiences;
- processes of active and participatory learning.

The direct connection between these processes and practical outcomes is, as yet, to be reviewed and reported upon, as time plays a significant part in the embedding of the principles into practice. However, it remains the fact that the emphasis and fervent belief in policy-informed change has led the entire venture of education for sustainability into an over-technical focus on structures and systems, which may be of interest to policy makers and academics, but remains beyond the influence and attention of most practitioners.

This disconnect between policy advocacy and practitioner response is perhaps of little surprise, and we might consider at least two reasons why this happens.

First, we have known, and attempted to respond systemically to the problem of change being non-linear and that, despite what policy makers desire and mandate, it remains the case that people do not always do as they are asked to do as education from the top down persistently fails to connect with the grounded needs.[4] The reality is that while the ideas associated with education for sustainable development may make sense rationally, for most people, and most institutions, it feels much more like business as usual because this is just one more administrative demand among many as they try to deal with their daily functions. What matters on the global stage with ecological sustainability can seem a long way from the pressing needs of the moment.

Second, the ideas, with the exception of the committed few, would seem to fail to connect with the day-to-day demands of the established and mainstream school community. The point is that the general education for sustainable development messages are either too close to what they already do ('We already work in networks of schools' or 'We already adopt a critical thinking programme'), or too esoteric and heady ('We don't have time for teachers to undertake action research, just tell us what to do'). Our examples earlier in this Exploration of efforts around the world, in quite different systems of educational provision, illustrate that when applied in practical terms the connections can readily be made and embed very easily into the life of the school – and considerably enhance in many cases the recognition and value placed upon the natural surroundings that exist around many of the school sites. But in each case, we see that when the fundamental organizing structures remain firmly in place, they illustrate our attempt to 'cope with the conditions of the twenty-first century with the thinking and practices of the twentieth' (Laszlo 2001), where responses fail to connect with the problems we face in a way that steps beyond a mechanistic way of seeing the world, rather than any real reappraisal of the meaning of school. We are, as such, schooled into thinking that our version of school is the only way we can proceed, and it would be foolish to think that this is the case. However, to consider any alternative case, instead of 'school', another school is just like the chicken and the egg problem – which comes first? In the context of this exploration, perhaps we are talking about a different egg, a different chicken?

So while it would seem that the education system is an ideal place to locate an agenda of education for sustainable development, it is competing with the day-to-day realities of schooling in the form of 'business as usual' and its close connection with the economic drivers of the industrial growth society. As a result, we might need to think slightly differently about the nature of the problem that faces our communities and schools as they grapple with the immensities of transition from one world of activity towards an as yet undisclosed alternative.

Instead of relying solely upon the systemic and the macro solution that are determined by policy makers, we are inclined to explore the lessons to learn from the micro, small scale and perhaps rather mundane activity that can happen anywhere that people find themselves. In responding to the unsustainability of daily life we can observe and recognize dysfunction where it exists and then make choices, and through such choices start to connect into the much bigger systemic picture.

This begins with awareness brought about by doing; we learn to see the issues through existing forms of instruction and knowledge transfer, but it does not stop there. As our ability to do things in response to an

Table 1 A shift from reductive to complex consciousness

From reductive understanding	Towards complex understanding
Passive transfer of knowledge	Understanding and getting to the root of issues
Teaching attitudes and values	Examining the narrative that informs attitudes and values
Seeing people's behaviour as a problem to be solved	Seeing people and their behaviour as the arbiters and brokers of change through their life choices
Managing the messages and conversation	Entering into dialogue, negotiating, and acting
Expert/novice styles of practice	Informal, flexible learning partnerships
Awareness raising	Changing the narrative which influences decision and action
Changing behaviour	Changing structures and institutional practices

unsustainable situation grows, so too does our awareness. The insights we gain enable us to refine our methods of understanding and our responses become more coherent and fluid, and in turn our eco-awareness evolves, through our daily practices, into what we can call an eco-consciousness (Table 1).

Evidence of these observations comes in the form of the plethora of initiatives around the world[5] that are slowly defining their own ways of demonstrating their part in a new ecological narrative. The problem we have, and it is an interesting problem to face, is making sense of these numerous initiatives. Such is the diversity and dynamic nature of human response – generating meaning from the sum of the whole, and creating a broader and comprehensible global narrative of eco-change – that it is a very different but just as potent a means of establishing a change process as that of policy-led reforms (see also Birney and Reed 2009).

While the specifics of the many and varied community programmes differ, they share a similar epistemology in that they question the prevailing logic of established systems and practices and are integrating nature into their design. They question the existing mainstream cultural approaches that differentiate between urban and rural, and instead they are forming a different alliance with our urban space. One where the practicalities of, for example, growing food can emerge as a vital part of the urban architecture, both in the reality of the growing schemes, and in the collective imagination; as it illustrates a way forward for the urban lifestyle that breaks from the industrial past. Some of these initiatives generate a clear statement of intent, and focus upon practical solutions in the light of available evidence.

> *For example:* The Transition Network (Hopkins 2008) which is designed to help communities deal with climate change and build their capacity to respond to the impending energy crisis, or Incredible Edible, which has adopted a strategy that uses local food production as a way of building resilience to broader environmental change (Clarke 2009a) and establishes a practical response to food security by growing food in urban settings. Experience suggests that these routes generate community involvement and raise public awareness of other environmental concerns and interests. These examples show how the simplicity of a single-issue approach can provide people with a way of connecting with what is otherwise a somewhat abstract education for sustainable development narrative. The focus, for example, of growing local food takes place at a scale that people can relate to, where they can see the practical impact of the changes they adopt. What is interesting is that through these actions, we have begun to see that people make the wider set of connections to global changes, and can understand the bigger story in more substantive terms.

Other projects that pursue similar environmental and economic change are more eclectic and nuanced but have the same underlying educational logic. A persistent narrative across the many projects explores how to proceed from where we are now and how to provide lessons that can be learned along the way. From the complex and powerful educational permaculture programmes of projects such as CERES in Melbourne, to the urban growing schemes on the streets of Detroit D-Town project and the rooftops of York City, to the huge twenty-first-century Eco-City designs being formulated in China to accommodate millions of new urban inhabitants, the story remains the same. It highlights the importance of the small examples, where a careful focus on the neighbourhood, the behaviour to the first Pop-Up-Farm network that I have been involved in establishing across primary schools in Lancashire and choices people are making, the way the places influence that behaviour and the examples that can both inform and guide help transcend the prevailing habits.

> *An example:* CERES is a not-for-profit, environment and education centre and urban farm located by Merri Creek in East Brunswick,

Melbourne. It provides an excellent example of how to rethink derelict urban space, built on a decommissioned municipal tip that was once a wasteland – today CERES is a thriving, vibrant community. It has over 300,000 people visiting the site each year. Many more connect with the organization through their innovative programme taking sustainable education directly to schools across the region. As an educational resource, CERES is recognized as an international leader in community and environmental practice, it runs the CERES Organic Farm, a market, a shop, co-ops and a café, and permaculture and bush-food nursery as site-based social enterprises which are each contributing important knowledge and skills into how new solutions can be used to combat climate change.

The centre hosts a range of community groups such as the Bike Shed, Community Gardens and Chook Group; each call CERES their home and are a vital part of the CERES culture. The centre manages all of its own waste and water on the site, and much of the site is powered by renewable energy such as wind and solar. It serves as a model for a possible future where innovation, sustainability, equity and connectedness are valued and taught through modelling and trial projects.

CERES is a good example of the 'other school'. Adopting the operational logic of working at the strata of society where it can begin to influence much greater numbers of people through direct and indirect physical contact, it demonstrates how school could now be conceived. Strategically, the traditional school is located at a crucial point in the civic society architecture and therefore is a vital player in any process of transformation. If it is to play a transformational role, then a significant aspect of that role has to be in the form of becoming the place within a community that ensures critical engagement with the vital issue of our time, an absolutely practical, economically sensible and educationally appropriate venture for any rational system that wishes to ensure its long-term viability and relevance to its users.

In attending to this ecologically focused agenda, schools might themselves be transformed into playing new roles within their communities, as educational facilities, libraries, resource centres, centres of excellence, food hubs, horticulture centres, arts events venues for conferences and public debates, and business and cooperative developments of all kinds. The direction of travel is clear; we are moving rapidly away from the old narrative of education that was servicing a core of young people towards the role of the school as something far more embedded into local, regional, national and international architecture of education for a sustainable community, an urban, learning hub, a farm for the ecological mind and landscape, a school of and for sustainability.

Summary

Our narrative of growth and improvement is founded upon a world-view that is no longer tenable. Instead, we adopt the logic that underpins a narrative that is available all around us, it is the logic of nature but we adopt this inside the urban context. When we consciously adopt and emulate life's genius, a 4.5-billion-year story of development unfolds before us, and we can see that it is locally tuned and responsive but globally connected and life sustaining. This forms the basis of a new ethos, one that takes us from the ego to the eco. It is founded on an education and training and is abundantly evident within ecosystems. This is the metanoia – a shift of mind, and the transformation, a shift of action and practice. It is at once a personal and a universal phenomenon.

In the next Exploration we will discuss how sustainability is therefore fundamentally a community practice, and we will demonstrate how community lies at the heart of the changing narrative and enables other sustainable capabilities to flourish. We will suggest that a robust understanding of community, and its contribution to sustainable living, lies within any substantive meaning of eco-literacy.

Notes

1 A theme explored in depth in Rees (2003).
2 'Reorienting education for sustainable development is still an emerging concept that needs to be clarified at the national and international levels, a process that must involve public institutions, universities and industry stakeholders' (McKeown 2002: 12–13).
3 Commonwealth of Australia (2009) 'Living sustainably: The Australian Government's National Action Plan for Education for Sustainability'. Environment Standards Branch Department of the Environment, Water, Heritage and the Arts, GPO Box 787,Canberra, ACT 2601.
4 See Seymour Sarason's (1993) exemplary study of the predictable failure of educational reform, the lessons of which are repeatedly not learned by policy makers working within a managerial paradigm.
5 As the range and scope of these initiatives is so diverse I suggest looking at the website associated with this work: http://www.school-of-sustainability. com, which serves as an up to date continuation of many of the themes, issues and examples raised in this text.

Exploration Three

How can community help schools to live with uncertainty?

> *Stories are the secret reservoir of values: change the stories individuals and nations live by and tell themselves and you change the individuals and nations ... Nations and peoples are largely the stories they feed themselves. If they tell themselves stories that are lies, they will suffer the future consequences of those lies. If they tell themselves stories that face their own truths, they will free their histories for future flowerings.*
>
> *Ben Okri*

Ben Okri poses the idea that our values are embedded deep in our cultural narrative. These values are like a subtext to our daily lives that, while they are not always present, serve as a bedrock to the busy activity of the surface, and as such they do not change very quickly. They are often evident in times of crisis, or when people come together over a great public celebration. They are regularly touched upon in political debates when concern turns to the social, economic and cultural consequences of our activity. But, in general, they remain opaque. This idea of something deeply held and slow to change powerfully captures the character of the challenge we face, as we stand at the foothills of the ecological problem, first in joining the powerful three – the social, economic and cultural – and then embedding into the collective psyche as a basic operational necessity.

Communities are hard wired to support sustainable living, and can be powerfully supportive instruments of stability during periods of change, because they hold within them the human resources of creativity and ingenuity that can be harnessed to demonstrate, guide and inform us of new ways that we might live in the urban habitat.

For example: My grandfather lived through the entirety of the twentieth century, an extraordinarily inventive time, but also an extraordinarily destructive and fragmented period in human history. When I was a young boy I loved to listen to him telling stories of his life, and his stories were always able to capture the importance in the mundane, constantly reminding me that ordinary people live extraordinary lives. By the end of his lifetime, my grandfather, an ordinary man, had lived just such an extraordinary life – he had travelled in both a car and a plane, nothing extraordinary there, but as he often reminded me, when he was a child there were no cars on the streets of his town and no planes in the sky. One of his early childhood memories was the day that the factory boss drove his new Ford Model T automobile up and down the streets to show it off to his workers. It was a remarkable story for three reasons: first because it was the first car my grandfather ever saw, second because the factory boss insisted on a team of men walking in front of the car picking up the horse manure off the cobbled street to ensure that the car tyres didn't get dirty! And third, because of the way it exemplified a form of society where workplace and home were closely aligned, the workforce lived in houses provided by the factory and the factory boss lived in the big house on the top of the hill. Everyone within the community had much the same point of contact, and the sight of the boss parading through 'his' streets, ostentatiously showing off his new symbol of wealth to 'his' workers was irksome, but not unusual.

My grandfather's story was ultimately not that of the gee-whizz technology, while technological progress provided some degree of amusement, it did not concern him. For example, he chose not to learn to drive but instead rode a bicycle until the age of seventy-five, he managed an allotment well into his eighties during a period when the majority culture was moving towards convenience living. He repaired things that went wrong rather than throw them out and purchase new items. He liked to know how things worked, and worked hard at educating himself to ensure self-reliance was maintained in an age where convenience started to override intelligence. What was of value to him was the strength of being with people, people to chat with, share ideas and stories, people he could draw upon in times of need. He saw richness in life coming through family and friends, he had a deep appreciation of the company of others, and recognized the value of interdependence and community. This understanding saw him through the good times and the bad times. Much of his working life could be defined by intermittent employment, with world wars and economic turbulence, unemployment was just as common as employment, so the constant of family and friends, community and kinship served as a foundation for life. It centred around what we would describe today as social networks, neighbours, chapel, school and, significantly, abundant food-producing allotments. His stories captured a rich tapestry of survival and resilience through these times, always optimistic, observant and intelligent. Not long before he died, I asked him about his life, and one part of the discussion, which I still have on a tape recording, focused on what he felt defined his time. 'Progress,' he said, after a pause for thought, 'progress can be cruel as well as kind, and we have to learn how to recognize changes for the better and avoid changes for the worse.'

My grandfather's stories illuminated the fact that the modern world has brought some fantastic successes. But in acknowledging those successes he drew short of assigning them universal acceptance as progress. In effect, he was providing wise counsel. As an observer of life, he felt it was important to consider the measure of our action. If the direction of travel was greater connectivity, and greater degrees of cooperation, then that has an ethical value which outplays the capital worth. If however, progress is defined solely through financial gain, it rapidly becomes a redundant idea. So the narrative thread of my grandfather serves as the basis of my thoughts in this Exploration, particularly focused on community and a transitional period where we migrate our activity from collective ego, towards a collective appreciation of eco. Once we begin to understand that nature demonstrates interdependence at a highly sophisticated level, we begin to see the way we are a part of our world, and how our connection with it is dependent upon the successful functioning of our own numerous interdependent systems. The relationship between these systems must be symbiotic, where one system connects with another but remains attentive to its own needs.

Describing community

Community is at once something abstract and concrete. It does not really physically exist at all, there is no specific place one can go to that would explain community, nor is there any one particular set of practices or ideas that successfully define what it is. However, what is quite clear is that the absence of one's connection into any form of community is palpable and detrimental to daily quality of life.

It becomes clear over time that any definition of community is always temporary and transitional. The notion of something fixed and solid simply does not make sense when we begin to consider something as dynamic and emergent as the web of interest, place, relationship and action that forms the basis of existence.

Community is perhaps best considered as a set of connections that weave and warp through a social setting, providing a continuously evolving structure for that society to operate within. The interplay between the different connections is forever changing and, because of this, it leads us to the opinion that community is fertile ground for transformation to a more progressive definition of sustainable practice.

For example, we might think of community as:

- creating the context for interdependence;
- helping us to understand and take advantage of networks;
- a place of continual, emerging novelty and creativity;
- teaching us skills of leadership;
- an expression of freedom;
- endorsing the power of local action;
- about knowing a place;
- challenging us to think again, it encourages critical consciousness;
- being timeless, and time bound;
- helping to make the connection between the global and the local;
- about systems thinking and systems acting.

Communities of any kind are dense phenomena. A central part of the transformation to any form of sustainable community is to recognize the depth and intricacy of relationships that exist within communities and use them productively to educate and inform (Capra 2005). It is the very density and overlap of connection that enables a community to become resilient, and the reliance of one part upon another works to its collective benefit.

The natural world teaches us that if we want to establish life-sustaining places, we need to nurture our communities so that they are richly varied and nuanced. These are therefore not static environments, they are hugely interdependent concepts, sometimes physically located, sometimes virtual. As a result they do not meet easily with traditionally conceived models of management and control; new ways of thinking about governance are required. Communities are dynamic, as they continually reform and realign themselves to evolve according to the situations in which they find themselves. The idea of the community as an ecosystem is therefore a helpful way to begin to examine our schools and to think about how we enable, or inhibit the natural development of community.

Communities are not planned, they are emergent, dynamic phenomena and, as such, they take unpredictable turns and routes as they progress and grow. Networks serve as a foundation for the basic pattern of organization for all of the earth's living systems. We see evidence of them in biological systems such as our brains, where networks of chemical reactions stimulate our thoughts; similarly we can think of our social systems as networks of communications.

In schools, and other knowledge generating and knowledge using systems, networks have become a major focus of attention. They are being explored for their possibility to transfer knowledge and expertise, provide support and enhance practice. The potential to extend them through technology is vast, it is quite possible to function as a network on a global level and still connect closely to a local community activity. There are also many informal networks within human organizations inside communities. Organizational theorists such as Wenger (1998, Wenger *et al.* 2002) have called these networks 'communities of practice,' in which people build relationships, help each other, and make daily activities meaningful at a personal level.

Within every community of people there will be a cluster of interdependent communities of practice, not to be thought of as singular, but rather as multiples. The more people are involved in these networks, and the more sophisticated and dynamic the networks become, the better the community will be able to learn, will be able to respond creatively to new circumstances, will modify, adapt to change and evolve. In other words, a community's creative impulse, liveliness and momentum reside deeply within its communities of practice. These considerations suggest that the most effective way to enhance any community's potential for learning is to empower its people to combine in communities of practice and learn together, following things that are of common concern and interest to them.

If the learning potential of a community resides within its numerous communities of practice, then we might ask the question of how these processes actually function in the many networks and communities it hosts?

The answer comes in the form of a system. We have to think of energy passing through a community in the same way as the sunshine warms the ground or currents of water flowing through a river. A community has to be attentive and respond to the possibilities around it, utilizing the flow of ideas and creative leaps to provide its nourishment, which in turn ensure that it can survive.

We like to think of this as 'playing' with novelty – a form of improvisation where being able to respond to novel and unlikely ideas generates a momentum of immense power within communities. Otto Scharmer (2008) in describing his work on change in organizations, calls this kind of phenomena 'emergence'. Emergence is a spontaneous leap of order at critical points of instability, it is an entirely natural process of change which we recognize all the time.

> *For example:* when we have worked hard at something for days in a methodical way and seem stuck, then we drop it for a while, go for a walk, and when we return to the ideas we seem to have made a breakthrough which was neither planned nor expected.

Emergence is a critical developmental element, as applicable to education and learning as it is to evolution. What emergence tells us is that we should embrace novelty as we learn to create sustainable community, it is the life-blood of creativity, it enables us to explore variety and difference and imagine new ways forward through our response, it is a fundamental of our natural world which we should embrace and learn from.

Understanding the importance of emergence helps us to see how its place within developments in community settings can inform our understanding of leadership. Whereas a traditional idea of a leader is a person who is able to articulate a vision clearly, and communicate it with passion and charisma, an emergent approach to community and leading within a community acknowledges the diversity of approaches people bring together to form momentum. The facilitation of emergence and novelty is really important in generating participation, interest, new ideas and enthusiasm. It is a way of leading that generates and encourages networks, creates a spirit of openness and giving, through which creativity can flourish. It becomes a powerful way of demonstrating, to all people who have contact with the community, that they matter and that they can participate in the way forward.

A further characteristic of using community as a way of leading comes in the way that it might experience periods of instability and uncertainty. The self-doubt, fear and confusion which often accompanies periods of uncertainty are important parts of the developmental cycle, and are precursors to emergent learning. During this time, old ways of thinking might begin to be replaced with new models and approaches. The resulting clarity can be enormously powerful and motivating but only if the community has supportive approaches which can be used at the same time; without these, people can feel lost and frightened and will return to earlier ways of doing things which are seemingly safer and less risky. Of course, not all emergent solutions are appropriate; the community that can learn to overcome single solutions and begin to explore more diverse solutions, and is willing to take risks and experiment, is a community that is probably functioning with a set of strong relationships. These relationships are another example of the interconnectedness that serves as the bonding material in a resilient group.

Providing opportunity for people to exercise choice, and to do so within a community of other people, is a liberating route to learning. We are essentially empowering their communities of practice not only to increase their political flexibility, creativity and learning potential, but also to recognize, value and respect individual dignity. A community that is capable of creating such conditions is starting to practise freedom as a fundamental capability. We are learning that if we respect life, and respect the life, energy and enthusiasms of others, we empower each other. This is the basis of emotional, mental and spiritual well-being.

Peter Senge (2007) observes that governments are 'muddling through', a strategy that 'characterizes most of us in rich northern countries. It embraces a combination of working to preserve the status quo combined with an almost hypnotic fascination with wondrous new technologies that, so the belief goes, will solve our problems' (px11. I). He suggests that this form of policy-driven action is misguided, even with the best intentions we have managed to create a collusion between government and local action where real purposeful connection with ideas plays second fiddle to a social and moral order wedded to consumerism, and to the old designs of modernism. Action is very different when released from simply implementing a service or product. Such action requires new types of 'people' skills, where we learn how to listen and hear each other. As we try to create more sustainable forms of living, we have to learn not to create a new form of the old economy where the sustainable lifestyle is a consumer product.

In a globalized world, where employees and organizations are able to be uprooted and assigned anywhere on the planet, the direct knowledge of place is perhaps of no immediate concern. Being uprooted is literal and metaphorical. But sustainability is all about place, it is about the connection with the earth. It is about the importance of the micro-contexts within which our actions have a direct relationship with the land upon which we live. Place is not a centralized question. Place is the habitat that defines us, locally understood and nurtured according to locally identified need. As such, the sensitivity of place comes in its connection with other important principles of citizenship, participation and empowerment through user-defined action.

Education for a sustainable living is an emancipatory process. It radicalizes people. It gets them to look again at how things are and ask 'why are they like that?' and 'why do we put up with it like this?' Instead of taking things as they are, and accepting that this is just how it is, we have to learn to challenge the existing order of things; only through critical analysis can we gain new insights and understandings. We have to be resilient to the inevitable resistance and refutation of the arguments that will come, but in the end we think that we can trust that these are ideas whose time has come, as Martin Buber put it: 'Listen to the course of being in the world … and bring it to reality as it desires.' We are beginning to know how to respond to the subtle forces that shape and influence our ways of being, by attending to them we learn more about ourselves and how we must change if we are to initiate any such change in the wider system. It is only through deeper examination of self in our situation that it becomes clear that the inner self upon which they draw seems to have a huge influence on the work they subsequently undertake and on its lasting influence. This influence is more than practical and technical in its form. It has something to do with the way in which real learning leaves an imprint that others truly feel in their own lives and work. It goes beyond the problems we face in our schools, it is a failure that persists deep down in our cultures across the many different, developed industrialized nations. Recognizing and then acknowledging the difficulties we encounter in living with uncertainty in both our personal and in our organizational settings heightens the importance of the need to think about and act in more interdependent ways; it may be one reason why we are so eager to belong, to join social networks and to establish connections with others.

My interest in this lies in the way in which an observation of interconnection can break through the veneer of the 'we' culture, and enable people to establish deeper and more lasting relationships to solve complex problems. In a school setting, for example, this poses some challenging thoughts: What would happen, for example, if schools started acknowledging that they functioned under conditions of considerable uncertainty?

> *For example:* Many headteachers and leadership teams have grown adept at presenting a united front to outsiders. This polished performance, however, belies an all too familiar reality, that the failure to acknowledge difference – that the 'we' culture of schools often portrays – is inhibiting their opportunity to transform working conditions. It might be more professionally and personally honest to think of the school as a place of a great deal of uncertainty. True, certainty is what the world might be asking of our learning establishments, but the reality is that learning is inherently uncertain. It is a difficult subject to examine because of its

embeddedness in specific organizational contexts and expectations. But in an environment of continuous reform in which we now operate, interdependence and honesty of fear about direction of travel seem to really matter as a way of overcoming enormous doubts and uncertainty about action.

A decade ago, we talked enthusiastically about the transformational potential of 'school' improvement. As our understanding of systemic change has grown, it has become more obvious that reform of an individual school community is simply not enough. It is clear that teams of people across a number of sites can generate greater potential and possibility for significant change. It is also clear that people need examples, pointers to use which can serve as stimuli for their own activity. Not surprisingly, when people come together to look at examples they default to simple solutions, often incorrectly. What we are perhaps looking for are route-ways to establish sustained, interactive relationships across multiple networks, a difficult but not impossible thing to do. The reason it is multiple is because to generate the type of organizational culture that can be resilient and remain relevant, we need to entertain multiple viewpoints. Not all of these will be the right ones to adopt, but organizationally our communities have to make sense of living with the ambiguity that accompanies uncertainty. It is these circumstances that generate greater levels of interdependence, but at the same time these interdependencies breed uncertainty, because new knowledge feeds the possible, they begin to need each other and learn that this need is more than simply about dealing with practical and technical demands of change, it is intimate and personal, it reaches deep inside their inner self asking them what do they really value. Placing trust in the potential of the larger group to be able to support personal need is a step beyond depending on someone else; it is a public act of faith in a particular way of working together and is not to be underestimated. Governments and their agencies are often keen to know the 'replication potential' of any perceived effective reform. While understanding this question, it seems to us that it misses a fundamental point about *scale*, *scope* and *stakes* of that reform. People working with each other generate trust and a whole social technology around risk taking, making meaning of complex situations and establishing practical solutions. These small-scale, localized solutions are extremely context specific, though; they are not something that can be manufactured by a demand to implement a reform from a policy maker. There are lots of examples of projects that have worked well in one environment and then fallen flat when efforts are made to put them into place in another. The message is not blanket replication, but a message of method, we need to study the patterns that led to the chosen solutions.

I recognize that this is difficult ground when it comes to our discussion of sustainable living. Do we watch a thousand flowers bloom, or do we deliberately intervene early and identify the salient characteristics in broad terms, and then encourage participation and continually refine the overviews to accommodate and clarify specific activity on the ground? Experience suggests that if we adopt systems thinking we can do the latter. It leads us to the view that there are some consistent, recurring patterns of activity that human beings undertake as they entertain ideas of sustainable living. They are not, however, perfect replicable examples; the local circumstance, what we might define as the social, political, cultural and economic ecosystems, play a very important part here, but there are patterns, something we will return to later in this work.

So we might have to look again at exactly what we should perhaps wish to replicate, not things that we do, but how we nurture working relationships that deepen interdependence. As Margaret Wheatley observes: 'I have changed what I pay attention to in an organization. Now I look carefully at how a workplace organizes its relationships, not its tasks functions and hierarchies but the patterns of relationships and the capacities available to form them.' If we can learn to see the organizational dynamics of social relationships, we can begin to model our interventions through greater levels of interdependence, at present it is not entirely clear if we have, as yet, developed an operational method which will enable this to work successfully.

> *For example:* I sit on a regional sustainable leadership forum for business in the north-west of England. Among the people at the table are the directors of sustainability at a number of significant regional businesses and strategic government offices. The level of agreement among the businesses on the core challenges we must attend to across one of the most urban communities in England is remarkably consistent. Where we sometimes differ, lies in the ways our own organizations might respond to these challenges. As we continue to work together and share our learning, we grow more interdependent as a group, but we remain identifiable as organizations. We have had to learn to communicate through a similar framework of concepts, and these have accelerated our ability to make progress on key areas of common concern such as climate change schemes across the business portfolio, and staff education and training for sustainable change. But the fundamental

connector is not as yet being considered, the link at the operational level of how we organize relationships. Until we do this, we will remain a useful group, but not an effective vehicle for change.

Community is timeless, and time bound

A commitment to learn how to live sustainably is a lifelong commitment that we pass on to others as we develop ourselves. This is what happens when people get together and actually learn together; from each other's questions and, from enquiring into specific issues in depth, they gain insights into their own understanding. In my work over the past decade, I have learned that time spent together, at inter- and intra-institutional levels, sharing ideas, and deepening understanding of different cultural and social conditions, enables people to further connect and relate to each other, can be extremely powerful, and has transformational potential. Time together, when it is undertaken well, can generate trust, and we take greater risks when trust is established and demonstrated. The time spent together is bound by the bond and intimacy of the moment of sharing and discourse, but the consequences of this bond extend far into the future actions that arise from this intimacy.

What will the impact be? It will be both global and local. The consumer mentality has brought with it an obsessive interest in the immediate, as both a consequence of an action or a set of actions, and as a representation of the only measure of worth. We live in a time that is obsessed with impact results and immediate solutions and, as such, we look more to surface and immediate issues rather than wanting to spend our time digging deep, examining the relationships that are at play, and how they are nurturing the environment for more fruitful ways of working to emerge. This reinforces our need to pay attention to scope – the connection of the local activity to an intergenerational set of measures that span beyond individual lifetimes. All too often, the measure of our success is seen in speedy, short-term changes. At the forefront of such change is restructuring, establishing what seem to be better aligned systems, ensuring paperwork is up to date, and keeping aligned to new policies. However, the shallowness of these efforts has led to superficial reform and meaningless, draining and futile action that saps human ingenuity, creativity and energy. It is not hard to get below the surface of any organization and identify the disease – the 'fragmentation' that arises from short-termism. Embedding scope into the community psyche is a strategy for permanence.

An examination of action, and method of analysis, can be extremely valuable in assisting communities to learn that real sustainable change is something that happens on both a local and a global scale, and that its measure of success has to extend beyond the moment. This means we have to think about the deeper consequences of what we do, and how their repercussions continue into an as yet undisclosed set of outcomes. If a measure of our action becomes recognized only if it succeeds at the holistic level and it is not seduced by the facile, it means we spend time considering the wider context, our designs improve, as our insights grow more universal.

When we reconnect self and system, we bring together the personal with the universal and we begin to practise sustainable development. The observation that across a community of people there is a vast, untapped pool of skill and talent is to understate the importance of having a chance to participate and to be a citizen with other citizens, engaged in common good. Clearly, there will be problems – community groups are notoriously tricky to work alongside, perhaps because they consist of such a diverse and divergent group of people who have no allegiance to each other except for the fact they might hold some common interest. This problem is magnified by the fact that western society has often sacrificed the universal in preference for the temporal self, and yet this pursuit of personal want, which is much more than personal need, has not resulted in personal satisfaction. It is seldom that the community can truly observe that all of the participants feel fulfilled in the things that they do there. More often than not, pointless restrictions and barriers that the organization creates serve to impede people's feeling of power and agency.

> *For example:* Sit down and chat with any group of people from any organization and pretty quickly you will often hear the same pained cry – we are doing things we don't see the need for, we are filling in forms which seem to take more time than the day job, our staff aren't listening, nobody has time for anyone else, we are always restructuring, we don't get time to implement one change before the next one comes along, our managers don't listen to our needs, they undertake consultation but it's a sham, if I could afford to I would quit.

Across the education system, the effect of working and living in an environment that is increasingly driven by outcomes is a feeling of rapid pace. A colleague recently commented that he no longer took annual leave of more than four days because he could not 'stand the feeling of being left behind'. Resisting the urge to say 'go and get a life!', he fully appreciated that it was neither wise nor healthy to approach his work in this way. Yet, despite being informed, articulate and in a position in our school system of some power, he felt completely trapped by the pressure of work. His predicament is repeated time and again. People know that what they are doing feels wrong for their well-being, for their families, for their colleagues and for their workplace – but they express a sense of powerlessness to overcome the problem and nurture a different environment. It seems that our sense of personal and collective agency has been sapped, the trouble is, while we might know this, we have grown used to waiting for someone to tell us how to get out of this situation and no-one, or nothing, is coming along to reform this problem; we have to see it for what it is, a systemic problem, and we have to act to change it. Sustainable development is systemic, it enables people to reconnect and seek wholeness, mental, physical, social and individual – to empower their lives and believe in themselves.

Summary

This Exploration has drawn attention to the importance of thinking about community as a system. At first this sounds like a rather strange way of conceptualizing something which often gets presented as a very concrete, certain and substantive entity, often linked to our established notions of organizations, as community brings with it similar associations. However, if we adopt the idea of system to the community concept, it becomes a more fluid, uncertain, emergent, dynamic and potentially powerful force for change. These are the natural conditions which could be used to define and interpret our world, more in keeping with the natural world around us. I have suggested that there are multiple ways in which we can consider this system, as an active living environment of ideas and practical solutions. These different facets can be embedded in the fabric of the community through visible examples which people can relate to, such as the growing schemes I refer to throughout this work.

Whereas learning communities can be located within the same paradigmatic frame as managerialism, attending and defining to the needs and structures of our organization of society, including our schools, through industrial metaphors; the locus of interest that we are now focusing upon is how a community can become sustainable, meeting the needs of people, and their environment. To do this we can usefully adopt naturalistic metaphors of growing, nurturing and seeding, as these project a different form of development that can begin to realign the collective consciousness of the community to function under different operational boundaries in keeping with the natural environment. An important focus of a sustainable learning community lies in its ability to establish connections that can nurture deep relationship within and across communities to achieve its goals. A critically important dimension of sustainable practice is to not rely upon previous ways of defining reality (through the industrial metaphor) and instead to be capable of using a language in keeping with the new ecological paradigm. In our efforts to begin to establish new methods of living sustainably, we are seeing how actions can serve as good starting points to prompt a new language of change. People can generate new links between and within the communities that they inhabit as a result of seeing work in progress, and as this happens we start to witness evidence of a new set of behaviours embedding deep into the functionality of our community psyche, it becomes in effect a new set of operational norms. The design that guides this is the natural narrative, the fundamental truth that we are a part of nature, not apart from nature. We are living beings pursuing our lives within a living urban system. It is the precise way this urban culture moves forward that is of interest, what is happening, and what could happen when these ideas are adopted, and it is to this that I will now turn.

Exploration Four

Open source living: when sustainability is *the* way of life

> *There is no middle path. Do we join together to build an economy that is sustainable? Or do we stay with our environmentally unsustainable economy until it declines? It is not a goal that can be compromised. One way or another, the choice will be made by our generation. But it will affect life on earth for all generations to come.*
>
> Lester Brown, Eco-economy *2002*

As our discussion has developed, we have been examining some basic themes of sustainable thinking, which concern:

- scale – planetary
- scope – centuries
- stakes – civilization,

and we might add

- speed – we need to act with intelligent haste,

to establish new conditions to sustain long term for community resilience and stability. We have also seen how these first two agendas feed to the third, a reappraisal of the stakes if we do not undergo the transition, the costs to our civilization. To get there, we need to adopt new models of knowledge transfer, and one interesting option lies in open-source practices, where ideas are free to users, with a proviso of feedback and participatory support. In all their many guises, these experiments with sustainable solutions add up to a renaissance of urban community, it forms the foundation for a new cultural and social movement.

In a recent article on the *Time* magazine website, Bryan Walsh (2011) wrote an interesting article on contemporary consumerism. Walsh says that after thousands of years during which most human beings lived hand to mouth, in the twentieth century the industrial economies of the West and eventually much of the rest of the world began churning out consumer goods – refrigerators, cars, TVs, telephones, computers and this changed our expectations of daily life, from one of scarcity, to one of plenty. George W. Bush won re-election as President in 2004 in part by proclaiming an 'ownership society'. The more ownership there is in America, the more vitality there is in America.

The ownership question is significant here, and the distinction between what we own and what we do not own, and what such ownership represents. Walsh suggests that even as Bush junior was announcing the birth of the ownership society, it was already rotting from the inside out. We might look at the start of its demise when the Internet company Napster began operating. The digitalization of music, and the ability to share it online through bit-torrents, made owning CDs superfluous. The Napsterization phenomena spread to nearly all other media, and by 2008 the financial architecture that had been built to support all that individual ownership – the sub-prime mortgages and the credit-default swaps – collapsed on top of us all. Ownership hasn't made the US or the UK or Germany, or Australia or South Africa vital; it had just about financially ruined everyone.

Walsh observes what we have already indicated earlier, that people were realizing that something was amiss with the economic model, and that a credit-fuelled economy was not a long-term proposition. By making new choices as a consequence, choices which are not mainstream responses and sometimes seem to be just plain counter-intuitive, they have begun to establish a very different way of consuming goods and services. He says that what is interesting is that some people are learning these lessons very quickly and changing their habits as a result. Instead of buying products and services outright, they are looking for new and different economically viable solutions. This is especially true for the young who will continue to bear the brunt of the recession, with a youth jobless rate in the US and the UK of about 20 per cent, and who have little available money to spend. Instead of individualizing purchases, they are pioneering a form of collaborative consumption: renting, lending and even sharing goods instead of buying them. You can see it in the rise of big businesses like Love Film and NetFlix, whose more than 20 million subscribers pay a fee to essentially share DVDs; or Zipcar and Liftshare, which gives more than 500,000 members the chance to share cars part-time.

Those consumer trends, while successful, are essentially Internet-era upgrades of earlier car- and video-rental businesses; they are revised and updated versions of an earlier idea. Walsh reports the underbelly of these responses, the abandonment of individual ownership, when he says that the really innovative spirit of collaborative consumption that is breaking the mould can be found in businesses like Snap-Goods, which helps people rent goods via the Internet. Or Airbnb, and we might add to this the couch-surfing and house-swapping schemes which allow people to rent and even travel free of charge. It does not stop there – people are beginning to recognize that renting is much easier than buying, and so schemes that let you rent a power drill via Snap-Goods or a local equivalent store for one or two days means less long-term storage problems and more flexibility of use. This is extremely useful in the urban context where storage space can be limited, and might explain why projects like the internationally successful Freecycle, where people post on-line items that they no longer want to keep for others to take away for free and use themselves, has become a massively popular local networking scheme.

While the individual projects are themselves very interesting, it is the underlying trend that is most noticeable. The real beneficiary of collaborative consumption phenomena, as opposed to the previous individualized consumer culture, is society as it mutates to what I will suggest is an open-source model of living. We will learn to give it away, share it for free or at least establish conditions on a 'neighbourhood deal' of trust and cooperation in exchange for a more resilient community base. In an era when families are scattered and we may not know the people down the street, sharing things – even with strangers we've just met online – allows us to make meaningful connections. Peer-to-peer sharing 'involves the re-emergence of community', writes Rachel Botsman, co-author of *What's Mine Is Yours: The rise of collaborative consumption*. 'This works because people can trust each other.' If we do not believe this to be the case, then consider ebay, the online shopping and trading scheme. We bid on ebay and we pay in advance of getting the goods, only a minute fraction of 1 per cent of all trades on ebay are defaulted, and yet we are buying from people we have never nor will ever meet, from all parts of the world, and paying them before they send us any goods, it is completely counter-intuitive to the established logic of transactions that the old system was hard-wired to maintain.

What Walsh illustrates is that we are trusting social beings, we yearn to trust and be trusted, and that this is a core feature of a community mind at work. He says, 'That's the beauty of a sharing society – and perhaps the reason it might prove more lasting than one built on ownership.'

Walsh's article emphasizes how communities can flourish through new micro-technologies of connectivity. Some of these enable people to generate an economic livelihood, some are practical solutions to the contemporary problem of urban living such as having little physical space, or simply not wanting the burden of numerous seldom-used resources and products (Leadbeater 2000).

Incredible Edible

In my own work, I have been able to experiment within a community project (Incredible Edible) to see how the simple idea of making a resource free to everyone (in this case free food grown in public places) can serve as a vehicle for radical thinking about design and regeneration of an entire community.

The findings from this work have subsequently prompted other projects, School-of-Sustainability and Pop-Up-Farm[1], which functions as a connector between local and global activities on the theme of sustainable living. Both projects have a set of small-scale solutions that are guiding day-to-day activity, and each functions to a greater or lesser extent upon open source and participatory development.

Incredible Edible is a deceptively simple initiative. It maintains a determined focus on food, through growing, cooking, eating and celebrating the food we can produce. However, to get to and from this focus we have learned that there is a need to encounter a whole set of relationships, of people, places, interests and activities that can be examined, and these can be used to illustrate a new way of living, 'treading more gently' as Thomas Berry (1996) says, on the earth.

The Incredible Edible mantra is 'if you eat you are in'; the approach we adopt is provocative and participatory, we anticipate participation but do so without exerting pressure – simply by existing as a project, people have migrated towards involvement. We begin to reconnect with our own relationship with nature, through food, and with others through the communion of food that exists in every person, in every place on the planet, but we do it with serious intent.

Our starting point for this food project comes in the redefinition of the use of public space, and recognizing that space is abundant in schools, in playing fields, playgrounds, parks and pathways. These are the starting points of an urban food-centred revolution. They serve as symbolic examples of how to reinvent the spaces around us for different use, drawing attention to such space and enabling people to participate in practical ways with visible outcomes and a revitalized sense of the possible (Arnold 1994).

We use a focus on food, food growing, food preparation, food preservation, food consumption and food waste management as a metaphor for our reconnection with the local space we encounter in our daily lives, and also to illustrate how divorced we have become from the food we eat. This is a simple, yet powerful sustainability story. It is through food that we flourish, yet we mostly place trust in the production of our food in the hands of very few producers and providers. This demonstrates in turn, how that dislocation, and the rebuilding of a reconnection, enables us to reinterpret our relationship with the earth, with natural seasons and with the track of time.

This is not sentimentality for a bygone age, it is a critical lesson of contemporary survival. Food illustrates graphically the insanity of our time through some startling numbers; in Great Britain, our food travels an average of 18 billion miles each year from farm to plate (HRH Prince of Wales *et al.* 2010). We are not alone, this is repeated across the developed world. In the USA, the majority of food eaten on a daily dinner plate travels more than a thousand miles from farm to customer. Food shortages have led to riot conditions in many parts of the world in the past five years. Access to good quality food is not just a problem of the south; in the richest country in the world, the USA, there are recorded food deserts (that is areas of housing where people live more than one mile away from any retail unit selling fresh produce) in both Detroit and Baltimore.

What gets this transportation of food to happen on a huge scale is oil. Oil is also the power behind agribusiness. Oil saturates every aspect of our food chain, but oil is a finite resource, and the era of cheap oil is rapidly coming to an end as it gets ever harder to extract from the remaining locations. Oil is also extremely dirty stuff, and as we know, burning carbon is not an intelligent way to see ourselves into a sustainable future. In the process of producing our food for the modern food industry we are polluting our own nest at a phenomenal rate. Our scale of carbon emissions is such that in a matter of 100 years we have managed to pollute the atmosphere with more carbon than at any time since the last ice age – carbon emissions and food are just one of a number of examples of the modern crisis; cheap oil is running out, and what do we do then?

For over a quarter of a century, there has been a slowly growing realization among people from many different social, economic and cultural backgrounds, that the way the human race is living on planet earth is not healthy for us, for other living things and for the earth itself. A recognition that the story we are telling ourselves is no longer suited to the world we live in, and that we face an urgent need for change. The urgency associated with these concerns was examined in the first two Explorations of this book, and we attend to the lessons learned in the form of the potential for change that we have residing in community in the third Exploration, where we have indicated why so many commentators are emphasizing a clear need for local and global action. We begin to see that the renewed interest in what is local is more than the stuff of lifestyle choice; it is the formative period of a new social and cultural movement. The idea of redefining community is therefore an important consideration in any new notion of practice, and it features strongly in many of the discourses of change, empowered community and redefined citizenship. A diverse movement of people and organizations is emerging from the rethinking of community, it often challenges the consumerist narrative and presents practical alternatives to the existing themes. These alternatives converge upon the critical questions of our time, how to learn to live sustainably and as one with our earth, using resources within our means and not depleting the very stuff we need to retain. In pursuing this idea, people construct a narrative of what it means to have a real connection with the world around us; it enables people to re-imagine a future where they play an important part, personally and in connection with others.

The way these narratives develop is through community – the connection of person to person, idea to idea, place to place, action to action – it is carried in the stuff of social networks. It is through shared narrative that we carry our day-to-day realities and understandings. These narratives have over the past centuries carried the rhetoric of tribalism, feudalism, religion, communism, fascism, capitalism and democracy to name but a few. However, in recent times we have been led to believe that one dominant narrative exists, the narrative of consumerism. This narrative carries with it values of affluence, individualism, wealth, lifestyle and industrial progress pursued without conscience or consequence within and between nations. This narrative transcends all of our established ideological boundaries. It restricts, inhibits and influences our capability to explore other ways of living by commodifying all aspects of our lives. It influences and informs how we see ourselves and how we relate to and live and work with others. But, in the end, it is just a narrative that has led us to a particular form of civilization, a story we are telling ourselves about the illusion of certainty of endless resource, continued economic growth at any cost (Orr 2009).

A living, learning example

Clearly, to move these ideas forward requires examples and workable solutions so that they become an antidote to the mainstream narrative, and by making them real and practised they do not fall victim to the accusation that the ideas are in any way idealist, elitist, factional or illusory. That is why it has been a central feature of the Incredible Edible programme to show people ways of achieving practical solutions as starting points to these huge challenges. When people can see examples of sustainable living for themselves, and build their own narrative and rationale behind their actions in the everyday and the mundane aspects of daily life, we know that they begin to migrate from their previously-held positions, they learn to adopt new practices. They might begin by being skeptical and hesitant, but with example comes inspiration and hope, and through hope comes a new perspective of the art of the possible.

The context that defined the Incredible Edible programme is complex: human beings are having a destructive effect on the global climate and we need to address the way they live and adopt new, sustainable reforms and low carbon solutions. Easier said than done! In achieving some new solutions, we need to experiment; through this experimentation we have recognized that people value and can learn from examples. They use the examples to examine ways in which they might make changes to their own lifestyles. When the examples are simple, clear and practical there is greater likelihood of success.

The consequences of seeing examples and subsequently acting on the stimulus of these examples are, however, unknown. People will take the ideas and push them in all sorts of new directions, so part of the challenge of Incredible Edible and projects like it is to ensure that creativity and imagination are continually fuelled and that connections to other projects are continually created. This is an interesting lesson on collective learning, it takes us from any pre-formulated approach towards a different epistemology framed around emergence and open-ended design. The sustained influence and inspiration for the programme does not come solely from within the Incredible Edible project or plans, it comes as a result of networks which we affiliate with individually as members of the Incredible Edible community. The range and diversity of projects with which we liaise is as eclectic as the members of the community themselves, and this ensures an array of interest and ideas from around the world helping to inform new and existing projects and plans. As a result, we have, as much by accident as design, created a platform for learning through the device of a project (both Incredible Edible and School-of-Sustainability illustrate this) which can be continually nourished and populated with ideas. While this might prove tricky to manage in the conventional worldview, it enables the project to become an entity to which people can associate their own meaning, and through this association they establish member-ship and a sense of participation. Whether they are physically in the project or not it can provide them with a point of connection and belonging.

Table 2 shows the Incredible Edible movement in the context of other movements around the world, and the examples with which we are in regular contact.

Table 2 Incredible Edible movement in the context of other movements around the world

Project	Issue addressed	Solutions
Detroit – urban farms, community gardens http://detroit blackfood security.org	Poverty and social exclusion, poor nutrition, vacant land as a result of economic decline.	Community food gardens; Educational programmes; Agriculture in schools; Promoting food-growing careers.
Greater London Authority http://www. capitalgrowth.org	To reduce London's carbon emissions.	Policy to promote green roofs and walls; Supporting Capital Growth campaign to create 2,012 community food growing sites by 2012.
Chicago City Hall http://www. chicagogreenroofs.org	Cooling buildings and producing food.	Use parks and the City Hall roof to produce food.
Cuba 'organoponicos'	Severe national economic shock and no access to oil imports.	Widespread organic agriculture in every available space in Havana; Organoponicos are commercial market gardens which allow the city to feed itself, and it is 60% self-sufficient in fruit and vegetables.

(Continued)

Project	Issue addressed	Solutions
Changi hospital, Singapore http:// www.greenroofs.com/ projects/pview. php?id=565	Provide healthy fresh food for hospital kitchen, to reduce the solar heat gain from the roof.	Rooftop hydroponic garden.
Farm folkCity folk, Vancouver http://ffcf. bc.ca/index.html	Aims to cultivate a sustainable local food system by working with farm and city.	Has established 3,000 community gardens by 2010 *Also*: 100 mile diet; Urban chickens; Protecting farmland; Supporting local producers.
Grow Sheffield/ Abundance project http://www. growsheffield.com/		Harvesting fruit from publicly planted fruit trees and people's gardens. Promoting where to buy or share local and homegrown produce.
CERES, Melbourne http://www.ceres.org. au/	To provide a model for education for sustainability.	A hub and demonstration centre for all activity relating to sustainability, food growing, energy and water use and permaculture.
Singapore	Various projects arising in hospitals, universities and the private sector to promote urban agriculture. The challenge is to maximize food production in small spaces especially in high-rise apartment blocks, to showcase and develop new technologies in urban agriculture.	Academics have developed systems for high-level apartment blocks based on ground-level and basement fish production, vertical farming on external walls, aquaponics on rooftops, and aeroponics in 'sky farms' between buildings.

Project	Issue addressed	Solutions
Ark Eden http://www. arkedenonlantau.com/	Ark Eden is based on Lantau Island, Hong Kong, uses its location as a world-class natural environmental wonder within China and Asia to suggest how its natural assets can be used to benefit education, local communities, Hong Kong residents and overseas visitors. The project aims to preserve the island's ecological, geographical, historical and cultural heritage by following a sustainable lifestyle and by providing inspiring educational and eco-tourism opportunities for children, adults, residents and tourists.	Interesting because it is a rain forest in the city area. It offers a range of practical educational and horticultural projects available to the entire community.
Detroit black food security network: http://detroit blackfood security.org/	As a result of economic collapse in inner city Detroit, citizens have limited access to healthy food choices, the Detroit Black Community Food Security Network has worked to raise awareness about food, where it comes from, who controls it, and the role it plays in building healthy families and communities. They have created models of community self-determination and grassroots citizen engagement.	A significant programme focusing on food and empowerment, particularly poignant for low income communities, this programme is a world leader in what happens when economic crisis results in significant collapse of existing infrastructure and people have to design their own solutions.

These projects provide a resource for our own ideas and initiatives, and they are sources of information on a wide range of benefits of urban agriculture, community learning and practical sustainable solutions:

- improvements to the environment – control of ambient temperature, improvements to air quality, biodiversity and habitat maintenance and enhancement;
- meeting nutritional needs of a population or neighbourhood and building and addressing poverty through community food production;
- cost savings – efficiencies in air conditioning, heating/cooling of buildings;
- risk mediation – preventing flooding and storm-water run-off, management of physical resources;
- social justice – empowering, educating and up-skilling excluded groups and enabling greater degrees of citizen participation;
- regeneration and crime-prevention;
- income-generation, micro-business design and alternative economic models for inclusive forms of economy;
- waste-reduction – food waste and scraps are composted, fallen fruit is harvested, soil is enhanced and better managed;
- raising environmental consciousness;
- urban green-space for amenity and recreation, well-being and establishing better conditions within urban spaces for future needs.

Making public space provocative

Along with Incredible Edible, these different educational programmes provoke public response in different ways, but retain the common thread of providing example and stimuli for new direction and interpretation of urban spaces and urban lifestyle. We have seen how physical examples can stimulate the broader debate on ideas of sustainable living, and how these physical examples slowly become the new landscape, which in turn influences a new mindscape of sustainable living and evolves towards a new reality of daily living.

Our work as educators is therefore a work of cultural change driven by purpose. It is to use and extend Michael Fullan's (1993) term, The *New* New meaning of educational change, the agenda for the century. How we become accustomed to the many ideas associated with sustainable living will have to be established through the commonplace, through the landscape that surrounds us. We will have to learn to adopt sustainable practices in every aspect of our lives, some will come through choice, but much might have to come through mandate, such is the urgency to realign practice to try and counter the excesses of climate change. We are more than aware that at the moment our built environment, our economic action, our transportation, our energy systems, our food production systems, our health and education systems are insufficiently encultured with the sustainability ethic but, again, there is hope, there is already some early evidence of change.

Incredible Edible is an example of this cultural zeitgeist in action, fuelled by the Internet age and viral networking. It has evolved over a relatively short period of time to become a powerful example of a way of responding at a community level to the considerable challenge of balancing our lives within the ecosphere. However, it is still in many ways an extremely fragile development and, as yet, rhetoric is far ahead of reality as it is only now beginning to establish some more substantive and long-term structures and processes that will enable it to build upon the power of the narrative which has been generated and in which so many people have an interest. As with all of this work in whatever setting, it is embryonic and emergent, it is recorded primarily so that we might learn from what we have done and share it with other communities who are interested in similar types of initiatives.

Question-driven change

The project continues to grapple with a few simple questions.

- How can we get a community of people to begin to think about their own environment, and think about it in more sustainable ways?
- Why might such an approach contribute to the transformation of communities, generating discussion and engagement in actions that can lead towards a more sustainable future?

In response to these concerns, attention is being given to new ways of growing food, rather than spending time on the big-picture issues which, in the main, individuals have little direct impact upon. These new ways of growing food locate the growing in the heart of the urban setting. This is done to graphically illustrate new ways of thinking about strategic infrastructure which can enhance the potential for reduction in the carbon footprint. If we are to make the transition to a less oil-dependent form of economy, and we are to maintain food supplies for our people, it is imperative that we establish new forms of infrastructure which can produce and distribute within local networks. But this is only a starting point, the essential ingredient in an infrastructure change that will move civilization to a new way of functioning. To get there, we have to ensure food security, as the food security measures will in themselves provide much of the ecological learning necessary for the transition to occur.

Incredible Edible is seen as a way of moving public awareness towards food-secure measures. Food security is a term which refers to the availability of food and the individual's access to it. A household is considered food secure when its occupants do not live in hunger or fear of starvation. According to the World Resources Institute, global per capita food production has been increasing substantially for the past few decades. In 2006, it was reported that globally, the number of people who are overweight has surpassed the number who are undernourished – the world had more than one billion people who were overweight, and an estimated 800 million who were undernourished. At the same time, Western societies are reporting obesity epidemics.

According to a recent Oxfam press release (2009), 852 million people around the world are chronically hungry due to extreme poverty, and up to a further 2 billion people lack food security on an intermittent basis caused by varying degrees of poverty, much of which is being associated to the impact of increasing levels of desertification of previously fertile farmland that is turning to dust because of climate change. As the price of oil becomes more and more volatile, farmers are turning to the production of bio-fuels to increase revenue as ethanol subsidies turn farmers away from growing food. The high price of fuel also places increasing costs for transportation and management of the food product, pushing process higher. As more people move to live in cities, and earn more money as a result, their dietary demands move towards greater levels of meat and this in turn increases the cost of basic grain, particularly in China and India. The availability of grain at a price that is affordable to people on low or poverty levels of existence has led to food riots in many countries across the world.

Community food security

Incredible Edible adopts strategies at the community level to establish an infrastructure conducive for community food security, a condition in which all community residents obtain a safe, culturally acceptable, nutritionally adequate diet through a sustainable food system that maximizes community self-reliance and social justice. It focuses attention on infrastructure at the level of grounded action, within communities of practice which are capable of having a direct effect upon people's lives.

Following are six basic principles of community food security, as defined by the Community Food Security Coalition (CFS), a North American non-profit organization:

1   *Low income food needs.* As with the anti-hunger movement, Community Food Security is focused on meeting the food needs of low-income communities, reducing hunger and improving individual health.
2   *Broad goals.* CFS addresses a broad range of problems affecting the food system, community development and the environment such as increasing poverty and hunger, disappearing farmland and family farms, inner city supermarket red-lining, rural community disintegration, rampant suburban sprawl, and air and water pollution from unsustainable food production and distribution patterns.
3   *Community focus.* A CFS approach seeks to build up a community's food resources to meet its own needs. These resources may include supermarkets, farmers' markets, gardens, transportation, community-based food processing ventures, and urban farms to name a few.
4   *Self-reliance/empowerment.* CFS projects emphasize the need to build individuals' abilities to provide for their food needs. They seeks to build upon community and individual assets, rather than focus on their deficiencies, and seek to engage community residents in all phases of project planning, implementation, and evaluation.
5   *Local agriculture*: A stable local agricultural base is the key to a community responsive food system. Farmers need increased access to markets that pay them a decent wage for their labour, and farmland needs planning protection from suburban development. By building stronger ties between farmers and consumers, consumers gain a greater knowledge and appreciation for their food source.
6   *Systems-oriented Community Food Security.* projects typically are 'inter-disciplinary', crossing many boundaries and incorporating collaborations with multiple agencies.

In each of these related principles there is a place for schools to take a lead role as they demand examples and leadership. However, at the time we began Incredible Edible, there was a great deal of discussion in and around education services about sustainable practices but relatively little action. We recognized that informal specialist networks existed which served as very useful starting points for informed debate, but the formative practical illustration was not as evident, and where it did exist it was shrouded in technical complexities which had a tendency to put people off trying things for themselves, or were presented in such a way as to suggest that it was too radical a departure from existing cultural practice to be realistically adopted into daily routines.

Local food security – the response

A few people in the project recognized that while there were efforts taking place at the macro-level to establish approaches that consolidated and connected the systemic management of food, it was at the local level that people would need to be engaged. In the UK, the issue of food security has had relatively little media attention, but this is slowly changing. Over the summer of 2009, the then Secretary of State for Environment, Food and Rural Affairs, Hilary Benn MP, published a report on the need to re-evaluate current food systems across the UK (HM Government 2009). Subsequent meetings in Westminster under the new coalition government and with the Commonwealth Foundation suggested that this issue was of sufficient concern to merit concerted international attention. The main focus of the then UK government response was on farming practices and potential changes to the ways in which farmers would reduce their oil dependency on diesel, chemicals and fertilizers. However, there are other, potentially high-yield responses to food security which offer a different response to food production, and of these the example of community response is perhaps most poignant and stimulating.

'Chance favours the prepared mind' (Louis Pasteur)

Incredible Edible started with a number of people being in the same place at the same time and serendipity playing its part. Our town had, like many other communities across the world, started to feel the effect of slow and sustained economic flight from the rural economy which continues to blight rural communities. The previous five decades had witnessed the slow decline and then closure of almost all of the local manufacturing industry, much of which was associated with the cotton industry, and the location of the town is not best suited to modern development and transportation networks. Local farming was in crisis with fewer and fewer hill-farms being commercially viable, the local market was struggling under the competitive pressure from the two supermarkets and the prospect of two more being built, and there was a feeling that the community was losing a lot more than simply an economic foundation that was focused around the historical market town. Many people in our community saw the decline as evidence of a continuing power struggle to stimulate and advance one form of economic development over and above all other forms of economic activity, and particularly agrarian economic practices. Having a fluid, responsive workforce remains a prerequisite for a capitalist industrial economy, as it did in the time of the land clearances of the nineteenth century. The detachment from land ensures that the people have no direct means of feeding themselves, and so become dependent upon money to buy food. This was both a deliberate policy of the recent past, and its repercussions and its cultural messages resonate to this day across all our urban settings.

> *For example:* Economic development of an underdeveloped people by themselves is not compatible with the maintenance of their traditional customs and mores. A break with the latter is prerequisite to economic progress. What is needed is a revolution in the totality of social, cultural and religious institutions and habits, and thus in their psychological attitude, their philosophy and way of life. What is, therefore, required amounts in reality to social disorganization. Unhappiness and discontent in the sense of wanting more than is obtainable at any moment is to be generated. The suffering and dislocation that may be caused in the progress may be objectionable, but it appears to be the price that has to be paid for economic development: the condition of economic progress.
>
> J. L Sadie (1960) *Economic Journal*, in McIntosh 2001: 94

While it was clear that our town was in transition from its role as an industrial northern market town on the border of Yorkshire and Lancashire, it was and still is not really clear what this transition is taking us towards. Earlier policy that had taken people away from the land, and from some form of economic independence, had now rendered many people dependent on forms of employment that were in themselves no longer tenable in a changing economic environment. This has created, in part, a group of people in the area who have no experience of work for more than one generation in their family structure, and no land available to grow any of their own food to support themselves. For others, it has meant commuting from the town to the city and this has increased the dependency on paid work, and distanced people who remain residents of the town from the day-to-day life of the place because their sense of place is now home-town and city.

The transition through economic need to work outside of the community in which one lives generated a gradual and yet identifiable fracture in what McIntosh (2001) describes as the 'ecosystem of place'.

An ecosystem of place relates to the ways in which people connect to each other through a deep understanding and relationship with their local environment. It is through this that they contribute to its cultural dynamic that helps to give a community both a character and a sense of collective self-justification. In effect, a practical relationship within a community setting generates a form of identity which has lived long in the memory, if not in the reality, of our community structures. Identification with a location, with its activity and its ways of doing things, is in part about being in a tribe, a group who share more than simply the co-existence of a location. The identity with place generates interdependencies. Just like any other ecosystem, an ecosystem of place is responsive and integrated with other systems, those which both influence and manipulate it in its functioning. These may be social as well as cultural and economic systems, but they certainly generate a powerful narrative to which people can easily relate.

What we tell ourselves is that when a community has a sense of place it is resilient and vibrant, it successfully provides for its inhabitants by generating a sense of worth, well-being and what Illich (1973) calls 'conviviality'. In such circumstances we might argue that an understanding of a local ecosystem of place has beneficial value in establishing an appreciation of the weave between forms of economy such as mutuality, reciprocity and exchange, and social and cultural actions through which people establish relationships and create lasting patterns of mutually supportive activity. However, in periods of economic hardship, and a period of transition towards a form of economy which is now much more interdependent and dispersed, relying not simply upon local transactions but upon economic connections on a global level, its ecosystem of place is much more fragmented, fragile and open to the same economic turmoil that afflicts any other part of the world. The transition is therefore of local importance if it is not to end up as drift, but it is influenced on a much broader scale than that which anyone can orchestrate.

However, this is not to say that people are simply hostage to 'given' or 'received' circumstances. People talk about change, they witness it happening around them, and they share their feelings about it. Sometimes this is simply to complain, to express a rather detached feeling of regret or anxiety or frustration; sometimes it is simply to express a feeling that something was amiss. Also it is an observation of the relationship between community and idealism and the fragile relationship that exists between individuals, their community and their feeling of personal and collective power to effect change which they cannot, in the end, influence.[2] This is far more than simple sentiment, it is a substantive sense of loss of identity and purpose which is as much spiritual as it is economic (Berry 1999, McIntosh 2001). In ecosystems of place, which are under threat, people have lost, and continue to lose, their sense of self, their sense of connection to a place, with which we think come other associated losses of community; self and local belief, and shared ambition. The identity of our town, like so many others, was becoming lost in the general anonymity of modern life, it was 'just another place to go through to get somewhere else'.

Historically, Todmorden has been a pioneering town of cotton mills, cooperatives and, interestingly, creative dissent and challenge. The memory of cotton and the connection of a trade across national boundaries that spanned the globe remains evident to this day in some of the impressive Victorian municipal buildings. The pioneering social and cooperative legacy remains strong in the many affiliations and self-help clubs that convene in the area, and the dissent is still present in the many creative professionals who take advantage of the studio space left as a result of the industrial decline. However, the resulting changes over the past 20 years in its population (from 22,000 in 1980 to 12,000 in 2008), and its subsequent impact on both local employment and infrastructure, had started to show in the way people responded to the place. Many of the signs were typical of rural decay and poverty, suffering an economic crisis of their own while being effected by the broader economic changes upon which they can have little influence. The high street shops that have been empty for months, the pubs that have closed, depressed house prices, restricted employment opportunities and the general feeling that there was nothing anyone could do about it, they were just symptoms of a systemic problem over which people had no control. It felt like we were on the slide and the only end-result would be something worse than before.

We describe these changes as a feeling of decline because that is how it was experienced. Living in a place for a long time generates an emotional attachment to that place, through familiarity of the air, the seasons and the climate, through memories and through relationships. An awareness of loss is manifested, therefore, in an emotional response; it felt a bit like the idealism and community, that must have been vibrant in the town of the past to create what it once was, had started to wane. There was a feeling of drift, anonymity and alienation in what was once a thriving and close-knit community and this makes one uneasy, uncomfortable and unsure. This undercurrent of unease and dissonance is not unusual in a border town trying to realign to a more urban form of life. Traditionally, border towns have been used to a steady through-traffic of people and with them came a tidal wave of ideas and possibilities. The town is no exception in its diversity of cultures represented over a substantial part of the nineteenth and twentieth centuries. In the past people had arrived and stayed; now they were not even stopping. What we were witnessing was the decline in the way that the place caught those people and embraced their contributions and provided them with a home in which they could consider the possibility of creating a living.

Growing connections – a model for action

When we reflected recently on the origins of Incredible Edible it was clear that there were a series of concurrent discussions in which we were involved that were taking place over 'futures'. Some were local, some were regional, some were national and some were global. These discussions held within them a similar theme – that the old way of doing things through local councils, unidentifiable committees and regulatory bodies was no longer working, nor representing our interests, but instead it seemed to have more in common with supermarkets and high street shops. In the words of the poet TS Eliot, we were '… no longer at ease in the old dispensation'. Indeed, our feelings were that we were beginning to witness the disease of consumption at all costs, which was leading to our collective feeling of decline.

In response, Incredible Edible's basic aim was to generate awareness of three core agendas for change:

1   Change in community behaviour.
2   Change in local business activity.
3   Change in awareness and knowledge of sustainable living achieved through new learning.

Our intention was to design a different way forward which carried with it a simple and powerful message which people could connect to, and which would be open enough for widespread participation and engagement without exception.

We envisaged this in the form of three interdependent agendas of community, business and education (Figures 2, 3 and 4). The critical connector was the local production of food. Food served as the catalyst for discussion and action to establish new ways to see and use land within the community, new ways of educating people from cradle to cradle (a term originally created by Walter Stahel), from the school through to colleges and into the local environment, and engaging local business in sourcing and creating new ways to connect to the community by growing new markets to ensure greater levels of local food production, sourcing and distribution.

Figure 2 Three activity plates of Incredible Edible.

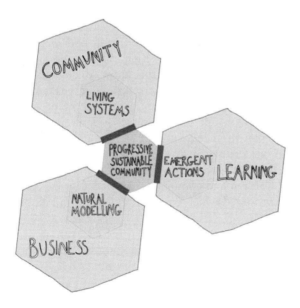

Figure 3 Example of the learning connections created from a focus on
progressive community.

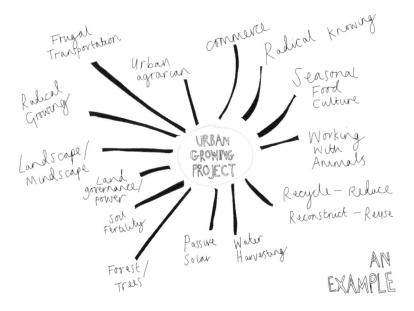

Figure 4 A range of connections we have made from a focus on food into
   emergent actions, living systems and natural modelling.

The connections between food and land, food and markets, and
a need to educate people to re-think their relationship with food
use and food production and to pass this knowledge to others was
our way of response to the wider, macro-economic challenges that
we were recognizing. Our project drew attention to the necessity for
a sustainable system to include an economic dynamic, but this had
to align and not inhibit the needs of both community and the broad
requirements that we envisaged any new learning would demand.
The connection, therefore, between business and community, business
and learning, and learning and community enabled a public conversation to begin to be fostered which continues to evolve and develop to
this day.

The example in Figure 4 illustrates the many and various ways in
which one focal point, the urban growing project, has stimulated
learning against a variety of themes which in turn enabled people to
establish working examples.

These examples can demonstrate to others the ways of establishing
individually identifiable activities in the form projects, which also link
together and can help to provide a set of connected systems for more
sustainable living.

Some illustrations:

An interest in frugal transportation could be linked to the distribution of food across the community, and generates a business link between the local ice-cream vendor who already runs a service around town street-by-street. Extending this business into a new connection of food through door-to-door delivery of food (fruit and vegetable) boxes.

An interest in fruit growing among a small group of people stimulated an initiative across the town to first identify possible sites and then to plant the basis of an urban orchard of over 800 fruit trees in just under two years. During the planting period, discussion between participants turned to the ways in which new stock could be established and over the autumn a further 500 new trees were grafted onto root stock. The group offered the skills programme to the wider community and a diverse group of people from across the town attended and learned the basic grafting skills required to propagate new fruit trees. This scheme is now offering training courses and is a viable small-scale enterprise in its own right; it is open to anyone across the region to participate and learn the skills required to graft fruit trees.

After observing that there were only two bee-keepers in the upper valley area, I placed an advertisement on the Incredible Edible website asking for anyone who wanted to learn bee-keeping to come along to a meeting to discuss possibilities. A year later, there are more than 25 regular members of the bee club, and eight active hives are located in a number of sites around town. The group has adopted some traditional methods, and is experimenting with some top bar hives which adopt much more natural methods of bee-keeping. The group membership ranges from 12 years old to 83 years old. Plans are underway for an extensive public awareness programme using sites around town to inform and guide public understanding on the importance of maintaining healthy bee colonies, their significance in the pollination process and their contribution to health through the range of by-products associated with the activity of bees. The project is about to provide school visits to enable younger members to begin to participate in the projects.

While we heard from elsewhere that more interdependent communities would have a better chance of responding resiliently in times of economic challenge (Hopkins 2008), we did not know if this was the case in our environment. So the simple focus on the growing and sharing of food to spread the ideas and aspirations of a bigger change came in the form of a re-established food-focused community seemed like a good first step to take.

This early formulation of our approach was pragmatic as much as idealistic. It was necessary to take a route that would lead to jobs as well as begin to raise awareness across the community of the implications of food insecurity, and to influence formal and informal education providers about a need to look again at their role and function in generating capacity for deeper understanding, knowledge and skills to generate food security. Food has always featured in our local landscape, we had grown up with local farms providing for us, and we had a strong tradition in the town of public allotments and private gardens, added to which the local countryside was an abundant resource for people to pick berries and nuts in the coppices and hedgerows. As such, food has always been there to serve as a connector, people understood the essential role it plays in their lives and historically people knew which kind of food grew well in the region and where it could be sourced. We were aware, though, that food has increasingly become something distant; the rise of imported food and out-of-season food had generated an expectation for easy availability, low cost and no questions asked. This situation does two things, it detaches us from an important part of identity of place through food, and it generates a belief that local production is no longer tenable, fracturing self-belief and possibility and making everyone more dependent upon the anonymity of market forces. The idea of security of food does not need to be in our design for our survival because we have come to believe, as a result of experience, that someone else will always supply it.

Growing connections: a model of action

One practical step which bridged the gap between talking about food security and actually engaging in something which created change that focused on food security started on the railway station platform. Herbs were planted by volunteers in the railway platform flower beds. People could get off the train at the end of the day and gather a handful of herbs to take home and use in their cooking that evening. We began speaking about the project at the different events we were attending, word of mouth spread quickly and the invitations to tell the story gathered apace. Then one of us visited France and was struck by municipal planting in rural France which included vegetables in the Council flowerbeds. It prompted the obvious question: Why not here? Over a period of a few weeks many of the odd parcels of land dotted around the town were identified and planted, with orchards of fruit trees and bushes, and a variety of vegetables and herbs.

Table 3 First six months of activity

- Sixty people attend first meeting to fashion a community food growing plan.
- Seed and plant swaps start to get resources together.
- 'Proper-gander' gardens established so people could have a proper gander at what was growing, take the idea home and do it themselves.
- £750,000 school food hub bid to the lottery was successful to establish a hydroponic fish farm.
- Incredible Parents project getting parents at each school to work in setting up growing beds for children to begin planting projects.
- Churches commit to provide land and support.
- Harvest Festival established.
- Cafe discussions and films on a regular basis.
- Doctors take a vote for herbs and an apothecaries' garden.
- Older people's growing memories are recorded and logged on website.
- Every Egg Matters campaign establishing a backyard egg production scheme across town, each school is involved as part of the scheme.
- Agriculture show – new growing section included in the programme.
- Community Pay-Back get involved and provide physical labour and time to establish the growing structures around town, by the end of the season 180-plus beds are located across the urban space.
- Incredible Buzz – a bee-keeping group is set up and 25 members are training in basic bee-keeping skills.

Within three months there were people all across the town participating in the effort to grow food, develop new networks to reclaim land and sharing ideas and knowledge some of which are outlined in Table 3.

Simple messages

People did the really simple things associated with growing, planting seeds and fruit bushes and fruit trees in public places, using school playgrounds to create community allotments, and making use of the health centre and the police station and ambulance service land. The High School, recognizing that it had probably the most available expanse of land in the town, recruited the help of the Community Pay-Back scheme and worked with Incredible Edible to build a large polytunnel. This structure now provides seasonal vegetables to the school canteen, and excess produce is sold in the town market. The school worked with the initiative to put a successful bid to the Lottery Fund which has enabled the project to plan to build a sustainable hydroponic fish farm on the school site which will be operational late-autumn 2011. This initiative is a joint venture between the school, the community and Incredible Edible. As such it had to establish a new community entity to ensure good governance of the financial and land resource so a Community Interest Company was formed. This company has representatives from the community, the Incredible Edible project and students and staff from the school.

The new community company arrangement enables the school to participate in a completely new form of learning venture, with close connectivity to the interests of people living nearby, those in the business community who want to establish a food hub on the site in partnership with the school, and draw down expertise to provide technical assistance through Incredible Edible from university students and staff who are experts in hydroponics, reed bed filtration systems and associated soil and water management technologies. All of these capabilities were previously unavailable at the school. In addition, they will offer courses and advice as well as produce for all the town restaurants and cafés. New courses in land management and rural ecology are planned for this academic year. Evening cookery classes take place monthly at the café. We have undertaken an audit of all the local egg producers, encouraging many people to take up hen-keeping and created an egg map for the town of local producers using googlemaps so that people could source their neighbourhood for eggs. Furthermore, the town centre has been mapped in such a way that people visiting can learn about different aspects of the sustainability plan of the town through participation in a 'green route'. This public display of community learning is attracting considerable numbers of visitors, which in turn has increased the footfall in the market and local shops.

This 'seeding of minds' coincides with our work being shared on the website to expand the network of ideas to others. At present the website has about 15,000 hits per week. As a result of the level of interest we launched 'Incredible Spreadables' – a learning resource to share the ideas in a more structured manner, and to be able to collect evidence from other projects to inform and guide our own learning. This has also generated another project, School-of-Sustainability, to cater for the developmental ideas arising from the international interest. Sharing this know-how has itself become a significant feature of town life, with regular gatherings in the café to show films and hold discussions on issues related to the wider picture of global warming, permaculture and other themed events, and a planned series of Royal Society of Arts (RSA) lectures is to begin Autumn 2011. The annual autumn national conference that is held in the town hall attracts politicians, regional policy advisers and planners, farmers, food company representatives and many members of the local community attend annually.

Response

The traditional establishment continues to find this difficult to comprehend and continually seeks to categorize the programme as 'just a food project'. Much of the early media presentation of the project talked of 'the good life', referring to the television sit-com of the 1970s. The fundamental point of people expressing in whatever way they could a frustration and concern for an unsustainable direction of economic, social and cultural travel seemed to be continually missed by many commentators.

Even more progressive organizations managed to fail to see the broader implications of the programmes radical intention. The Federation of City Farms and Community Gardens, in their classification of different types of community project, have termed Incredible Edible a 'local food coalition', meaning a group of organizations working together to create a local food system.

While this gets a little closer to the agenda of Incredible Edible, it missed the sustainable element. Part of this sustainability comes, as they indicate, through partnership. It remains a very important element of the Incredible Edible process that this work is about people, relationships and place, the way we connect to where we live, and the way we relate to each other all matter immensely, otherwise we fall foul to the managerial models which define how to live for us, and determine what, where, when who how and why we do what we do. This is ultimately a progressive project that is articulating social empowerment with social and cultural change; it should not be underestimated that this message has far reaching implications that transcend regional national barriers and connect across the world to people of all colours and all creeds.

The Incredible Edible approach is grounded in an asset-based community development model. This means that any community should approach regeneration using the resources and assets available to them, in contrast to a needs-based approach. In any community, there will be a set of resources to harness. IET focuses on partnership working, choosing the path of least resistance, and using what's locally available, but this asset issue is vitally important as it enables real economic resource to be established within the heart of the community, through which intergenerational aspiration can be embedded, people can use the project to see that they are setting up conditions for the future of the town for their children and their children's children. This is not dissimilar to the formative period of Todmorden, when the Victorian infrastructure was created and which people today still recognize, use and value.

We have continued to learn the obvious, that food is a great connector. The simple act of growing food has a resonance with people from every corner of the community, it is so easily accessible and the benefit of this simple message magnifies season upon season. It also enables people from wider afield to connect into the narrative. People visit the project and bring their own examples and stories, this enables a much more extensive, relationship-based network to emerge. It was not necessary to orchestrate 'community outreach' meetings or similar ventures because people simply turned up and joined in. As people participated, we have been concerned to ensure that new perspectives and suggestions are engaged with and supported as much as possible. It is clear that not every idea will work, but how do we know which one's until we try?

> *For example:* it was suggested that the initiative should be opened up to include young offenders involved in Community Pay-Back. Their enthusiasm and pride in the project has seen them building polytunnels, planting areas and they are now a vital part of the digging and laying infrastructure across town as the care homes, the old people's centre, the schools, the health centre, the various cafés and eateries, the local police station, the social housing programme, the services such as bus shelters and railway platforms and car parks are utilized as resource. In turn, these individual locations generate pockets of interest and enthusiasm, and contribute to the cumulative impact across the town of the initiative as we can point visitors and media to witness the work first-hand.

Furthermore, we have noticed that people make wider connections to sustainability thinking. They do not see Incredible Edible as a single-issue project. Our most pressing problem is that the success of the project has meant people think that it is fully staffed with paid employees, whereas the project is run almost entirely through voluntary activity. A recent meeting in a town centre café showed a film about peak oil and over 70 people attended, many from town, but also people from other neighbouring communities. Two hours after the film finished the room was still full, nobody had gone home, and it was alive with discussion in response to the film, and what relationship it might have to things we were doing in our own setting. The repercussions are still being thought out as we meet and reflect further some ten months later. This connection beyond the basic idea of the Incredible Edible initiative serves to strengthen the enthusiasm and engagement of participants. It is reinforced further by recognition from national organizations, and through the multiple film crews and news reporters from around the world who have opened a conversation within and beyond the town extending across the planet. We use the website to generate links and to seed the deeper message about sustainable living.

The use of public land is highly controversial and contested, land has historical ownership which often combines with power being exercised by one group over another to secure and maintain rights of access and use. It was somewhat predictable that the local authority would have problems with citizens planting on Council land, including school land. However, after a number of meetings where the Council raised concerns over safety and purpose of the work of the initiative, and where we reassured and illustrated both the actual and potential benefits for health, community well-being, and the press and publicity opportunity of a series of positive reviews and awards from both regional and national organizations (Market Towns Initiative winners and Sustainable Development Commission Breakthroughs for the twenty-first-century winners) the Council has made a significant change to the legislative process which enables people to identify and 'land bank' areas for public growing of food. This change in the way that the local authority responds to the initiative is evidence of a broader issue, that the relationship between local authority and community can be redesigned to enable rather than restrict the activities of the communities in their care.

Incredible Edible has been successful in harnessing local assets and building partnerships, which is an efficient use of resources, and builds pride by focusing on strengths not weaknesses. This reflects the international asset-based community development movement.

Outside Todmorden, there remains a perception that it is not replicable, but this is changing as more towns adopt the model and as the project matures. We now have the evidence to show that it is, as new projects calling themselves Incredible Edible at city level as well as small neighbourhood projects, adopting very similar aims and principles are establishing both in the UK and overseas. It is clear that the concept of Incredible Edible transcends the local, it is of universal concern that we attend to new ways of living sustainably, and clearly solutions will come from all quarters, government, business and community. The Incredible Edible experience shows that converging these different groupings can be extremely powerful as a way of generating interest, initiative and solutions. While individuals clearly matter, because we are concerned about people and their welfare, this type of project does not just depend on the passions of a few individuals, but is a cross-cutting movement that brings together local agencies and groups around a common theme of action.

Self-sufficiency in food may or may not be the ultimate aim of a sustainable way of life, but it provides a topic for debate and a focus for thinking about the local context and how a town might produce more permanent forms of food supply within the broader context of challenge resulting from climate change. The human and economic resources of the town have begun to be harnessed, now it is time for a longitudinal consideration of the culture change that might result from such work.

Incredible Edible recognizes that the activities that they adopt are often in themselves rather innocuous, they don't seem to demonstrate much more than people can still grow plants, and can do that wherever they manage to put them. But we have come to recognize that these single small acts were symbolically important, as they represent a reconnection with the power to do something in a community setting, outside of the existing boundaries between individual landspace and public landspace. People were looking at the available public land and reclaiming it to make it more productive. In doing this they exercise choice, public action, civil responsibility and, because it involves others, they are actively creating communities of action.

All these elements of scale, scope, speed and stakes are replicable elements of a story, since they are about tailoring actions to local circumstances – 'Use what you have to secure what you have not'. Incredible Edible is simply the brand that pulls the town towards a focus on one aspect – sustainable food systems.

Summary

Incredible Edible is a locally responsive, universal model, displaying some important and possibly transferable characteristics:

- optimizing assets for intergenerational awareness and for establishing long-term structural conditions for community cohesion;
- drawing upon a collective conscience, or convergence of various concerns, motivations, skills and ideas through a simple message;
- communicating the universal – we all need food, it is enjoyable and can inspire people to think again about what they eat, how they get their food, and why it is important to make informed choices;
- looking to become resilient in the face of rapid environmental, economic and social change;
- forming a focus through which people can imagine, hope and be creative.

A significant feature of the early success of the project has been the way that the project places an idea in front of people with which they can easily connect, namely to rethink the way that public space is used in an urban setting. The numerous initiatives that have emerged from the basic idea, including connections to other similarly configured projects elsewhere, raises some important issues about what we are learning about emergent sustainable practice, and how this can be synthesized and used to inform future developments in this field. A central feature of this comes in what might best be described as open-source sustainability – where solutions are made readily available through networks and social connection on a global to local basis. This is an exciting and transformational development, not orchestrated, not managed or defined centrally, but capable of considerable speed of effect, transferability and nuancing to unique settings, and continually evolving and emerging as a set of both practical and theoretical explorations. Observations arising from this serve as the basis of the next Exploration.

Note

1 Pop-Up-Farms challenge us in unexpected ways and in unexpected places, showing us how easy it is to make little changes that make a big difference, so that we start to change our habits and behaviour and tread more gently on the earth. For more information see www.pop-up-farm.com.
2 This is a theme taken up by Kirschenmann (2010) in his extensive discussion of ecological consciousness and conscience.

Exploration Five
Can we create schools of sustainability?[1]

When I make a work I often take it right to the edge of collapse, and that is a very beautiful place to be.

Andy Goldsworthy

It is not necessary to develop the community through new buildings or changed priorities imposed through government reforms. What is needed is a new attitude within the various communities that make up any place. This attitude might best be described as an oxymoron: *communal self-reliance*. As I have argued, however, this is not to maintain business as usual, it is to ensure a sustainable methodology lies at the heart of this self-reliant community ethic. Where practised, and connected into specific places, communal self-reliance enables people to work together to question existing practice, establish and maintain relationships, and develop these relationships in the pursuit of common interests to establish meaningful connections between things which people wish to change. Until now, those attitudes have established the modern urban mindset, a mindset which, as has already been rehearsed, is unsustainable. The unsustainable urban mind has created a matrix of interdependencies to become what it is. Even when the intention is not to be unsustainable, the consequence of the interdependencies results in that outcome.

However, because a community is a social construct, and the connections within it are social and cultural as much as economic, its interdependencies can be manipulated and changed (Gribbin 2004, and Cohen 1993). They come in the form of individual engagement, through connection with ideas and shared interests. We know that it is through collective action in the pursuit of new freedoms (the things we fervently want to see happening) that change can happen. As Amayrta Sen (1999: 18) argues: 'Greater freedom enhances the ability of people to help themselves and also to influence the world, and these matters are central to the process of development.' This is helpful as the broad pursuit of freedom enables us to innovate and imagine something different. So a sustainable communal self-reliance can challenge the orthodoxy of existing community, evidently so in the example of Incredible Edible. What I want to do in this Exploration is describe some of the critical capabilities that we might aspire to generate through an educational process that redefines, in turn, community and education in the urban mind.

I have suggested that community acts as a capturing device that can be drawn upon to guide and inform and model behaviours. A place which captures a set of capabilities that we can learn (Sen 1999) – a place where we depend upon each other to generate understanding, engagement and participation, and through which we can learn to respond to social, environmental and economic challenge (Putnam 2000, Orr 1994, Soros 2008). *Communal self-reliance* functions as the manifestation of a set of capabilities within and between communities of connection, communities of place, communities of interest, and communities of action – all of which connect to establish a way of living (see Figure 5).

Historically, the school is located at the interconnect of a set of capabilities that serve to enhance or sometimes impede the growth of a community. However, increasingly, we are seeing that the school is one player among many, operating within the wider social context of a community.

To help us with this narrative I intend to proceed with a view that schools will remain significant within the communities in which they operate, at every stage of education from kindergarden through to the end of high school. However, their function is considerably more free-forming than earlier versions of school. They will be conceived differently to that which we have grown accustomed. Our guide as to their operational activity will be the development of sustainable community as a primary educational goal, and therefore we place community as a general grouping at the heart of the educational effort (Figure 5). School will then play a role in supporting that goal, but will not be the only participant in the educational effort. For example, we might be better to think of 'school' as something akin to the dynamics of the CERES project in Melbourne illustrated earlier, where business, creative arts, cooperatives, cafeterias, markets and self-help groups all convene on a site and use the resources therein.

> *For example:* we can take the urban farm concept and locate it into a school environment. We begin to look again at the land space around the buildings, we begin to think about the amount of

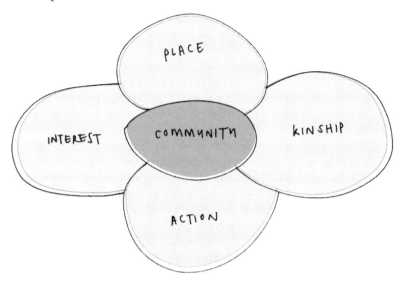

Figure 5 Community – place, action, interest and kinship.

tarmac, perhaps a grassy field, and a few bushes? What else could this space become? We can look at the site as a set of experiments in urban growing. We can see how there are some basic patterns of activity we must attend to – for example: the way that water is managed – we begin to think about the possibilities of the urban school setting as an ideal location for communities to focus upon and rethink in the form of learning spaces for urban growing schemes. Whereas globally we might discuss ways in which our local project urban farm plays a small part in the global need for food security schemes, an interconnection comes through the shared theme of food. The reference points however are different, one being structural (global concern for food security) and one cultural and social (local community growing scheme).

Since our world is increasingly connected through cultural, economic and technological mechanisms, and proportionally ever less physical, the meaning of 'local' is not geographical, at least not only geographical. It explores the ways in which flows of ideas combine as communities in the form of practices, theories, possibilities to be realized as forms of wealth, as environmental capital, human capital, social capital, spiritual capital, creative capital, and financial capital (Clarke 2009b, Porrit 2009) – the flow is between people sharing and playing with these things both in real time together, separately and at times virtually in their own time.

A community of connection

While the twentieth century is now well behind us, we have not as yet learned how to live, yet alone think in terms of actions and relationships, in the mindset we might need for life in the twenty-first century. This should not be all that difficult, as the dominant ideas of the economic and political model from the twentieth century have clearly just fallen apart around us in the past two decades and the lessons are there for all to see. These models have until now been looked upon as mutually exclusive: the failure of Soviet state socialism in the 1990s, and now Western market-driven capitalism have both defined, in their own ways, the failed ideologies of national systems. However, as Hobsbawm (2009) argues, both are 'bankrupt ideas' when we contemplate our futures. We need a progressive model to transcend the old order and respond to the new situation in which we find ourselves.

One particular feature of both of these 'bankrupt' models is the reliance upon institutions to perpetuate old-order ideological viewpoints, instead of looking to the new learning and understanding we might usefully adopt from our new technological advances and our increasing knowledge of nature. Ivan Illich (1973) argued that modern societies across the industrialized world appear to create more and more institutions, and that the consequence of them is that we live our lives in ever more institutionalized ways. This makes it difficult for people to challenge the existing order of things, or to suggest and to have taken seriously the idea that there are alternative ways of progressing. 'This process undermines people – it diminishes their confidence in themselves, and in their capacity to solve problems … It kills convivial relationships. Finally it colonizes life like a parasite … that kills creativity' (Finger and Asún 2001: 10). A counterbalance to the debilitating effect of institution lies in community, particularly a sustainable learning community, as it is capable of developing the capacity to be both self-reliant and, through the relationships generated by community, inter-dependent.

Institutions do other things too. They create experts. In *Medical Nemesis* (Illich 1975) the book began, 'The medical establishment has become a major threat to health' (ibid.: 11). I maintain a similar argument, that the educational establishment has become a major threat to learning (Clarke 2008, 2009c). The case against expert systems is that they produce a form of damage which outweighs the potential benefits they offer, because they obscure and collude with the political conditions that render society schooled but ill-educated, and they perpetuate the idea that people are unable to act for themselves. They diminish the power of individuals to learn and value their personal and social experience of learning themselves the means by which they might shape and improve their own community.

This problem of expert systems becomes particularly acute when there is a need to redefine the relationships that exist between school and community. Here, the institutional boundaries and structures can compromise the institutional potential to learn from the community, its default position being that the school educates the community and not the other way around. Despite plenty of examples that refute this claim, particularly coming from recent changes in communications technology (Leadbeater 2000), the underlying cultural message from schools remains the same, 'we know how to educate, and you don't know, so learn from us'.

As a result, community and school are stuck in a perpetual cycle of dependency of the worst possible kind, one where professionals and the schools in which they work tend to define the activity of learning as a commodity they call education, 'whose production they monopolize, whose distribution they restrict, and whose price they raise beyond the purse of ordinary people and, nowadays, all governments' (Lister in Illich 1976), and the community receives the product. Extending an earlier notion of schooling, it might be suggested therefore that people are conditioned to believe that the self-taught community is being discriminated against; that learning and the growth of cognitive capacity, require a process of consumption of services presented in a planned, a professional form (quoted by Gajardo 1994: 715; our insert of community) In this way, learning is a commodity rather than an activity, so any way in which a community might attempt to engage with a school is inhibited by its inability to present a form of knowledge to the school in a recognizable and therefore acceptable professional manner.

Institutions and institutional practices would appear to be addictive. The fact that school is perceived to be compulsory may be significant here – as institutions, schools generate habitual activities and rituals and these are difficult to quit once people get hooked on the idea that they are the only way to behave or to solve existing problems. If, as individuals and communities, we can develop the capabilities to distinguish between what we want and what we understand to be a requirement, we can use such capability to make proactive choices acting as agents rather than consumers of learning.

Having grown conditioned to schooling of a certain type (Orr 1994), to overcome the challenges we face from economic and ecological meltdown demands the cleverest of inventions, the smartest of technologies and the most politic and decorous of societies. The current landscape of challenges offers immense potential for people to work together in new ways to form new types of economic well-being which serve both personal and societal needs.

By challenging the process of institutionalization, by questioning the established notions of expertise and experts, and by critiquing the idea of learning as a form of commodity, we should be able to move towards a way of living and working in our communities where collective wisdom is captured and focused with clarity and purpose and without the embedded issues of ownership and power getting in the way; where people have a clear sense of the purpose behind the initiatives which serve self and others and, indeed, the well-understood needs of the community as a whole (Friere 1992).

A transition in thinking about how to live in the twenty-first century that redefines wealth in the form of environmental capital, human capital, social capital, spiritual capital, cultural and creative capital, manufactured capital and financial capital needs mediation. Our capabilities follow: schooling for sustainability would support activity that encourages the learner to consider the way in which these wealth forms are unsustainable, but could be changed to take a new direction.

A 'community of connection' that develops capabilities to appreciate and engage with alternative solutions, designs and opportunities and which values the very process of connecting meaningfully with others, helps us to think differently and enables us to respond to the economic-ecological, or eco-eco (Kelly 2009), demands of the twenty-first century. This model of community serves as a frame for thinking about the contributing factors which inform a dialogue for transforming the relationship between community and school.

A community of place

In a similar way to the failings of the macro-system, the micro-level is not without its problems (Klein 2001). While state-led reform of 'communities' continues to illustrate systemic failings through the alienation and disengagement of the majority of those this hoped-for reform is intended to assist, other equally problematic issues arise when the alternatives being pursued are for self-sufficient purposes. As an idea, the notion of self-sufficient communities has done just as much harm as good. It perpetuates the 'otherness' of those beyond one's own clique, and it generates economic inequality just as efficiently as any macro-market-led solution. The self-sufficiency argument extends now into our current school model. While defined primarily through school choice, it is just as much about exclusivity and self-sufficiency. Academies, Trusts, Free Schools and Foundation Schools are quite possibly the next failed extension of the industrialized, individualized cultural obsession with privacy and isolationist solutions to large-scale problems. They are the macro-solution to the micro-challenge and they perpetuate the myth that a new building with a new name (Academy, Foundation, Free School) will redefine the relationship between it, as an institution, and the community which it serves. 'We don't need you, we are self-sufficient, we generate our own solutions' is as much a lie as that which argues that we can only make cultural, environmental and economic progress with government. The message is clear, there is no dissectible self; we depend on each other.

It is therefore a maturation towards some other form of interdependency, one which connects rather than dissects self from community and from wider networks (Fielding 2001), that we urgently need to develop and the enquiry into the capabilities of sustainability take us in that direction.

So a community of place is particularly important as a way of making sense of the important role school plays within a social context. When one's environment has a 'sustained and lasting human value' (O'Sullivan 1999: 245) the result of the individualized and commodified version of globalization, rootlessness, transitoriness, and dispossession become more and not less transparent. The dependence by people on a community of place becomes in itself a value. Place is often cited as a significantly important feature of schools in locations of economic disadvantage, where, in the best examples, students are embedded into activity which helps to develop capability in the forms of environmental capital, human capital, social capital, spiritual capital, creative and cultural capital, manufactured capital and financial capital. However, just as the community of place can be a physical reality, it can also demonstrate capability in the form of a virtual reality. Take, for example, the degree of interest people have in Twitter, Facebook and other social networking sites.

Our capability to create and maintain a sense of place within a community – school relationship therefore explores both physical and virtual realities. To be successful it needs to generate capabilities which reposition the importance of a sense of identity, a need for love, care, protection, affection, understanding, participation, creativity and friendship.

Community-as-interest

Community-as-interest is demonstrated through the variety of ways in which ideas emerge and are seen to stick within a network of people. Examples of community-as-interest are as diverse as human experience wishes to take them. They are the nurseries of imaginative possibility, essentially important for the evolution of human activity from where and what we are, to where and what we might become.

A community of interest might emerge through an enquiry based on questions such as: How do we begin? What do we want to change here? Why is this proving difficult? Could we adopt a new approach to this work? These are questions often asked by people who want to experiment with ideas such as those we have been examining in this book, and want to embed them into their own environment. My answer is always to begin from where we are, to see that we have a rich resource of people available and that they are quite capable of imagining and creating something different. We then proceed to follow a set of activities which are designed to prompt new insights and observations of familiar settings.

> *For example:* asking the question 'What are you trying to change?' often results in detailed reporting of the many and various systems and structures that have been established to tell an external authority about internal performance. In contrast to this, I work with a staff group to reflect on these somewhat formulaic responses, asking why does this form of reporting have precedence over other ways of defining the quality of your work? Often the discussion identifies the way that people feel accountable to other organizations which on a day-to-day basis have little or no relationship to their own functioning. Revealing the hidden power of authoritative bodies, and then realigning internal mechanisms of power and authority, provides a space for new approaches to the questions and new solutions to emerge. We then begin to establish questions of value related to the internal conditions and aspirations of the school community, effectively asking what are we really interested in doing here? Once we reach this point in the conversation, we break for a week or so to give people time to reflect and identify their response. A subsequent visit would often involve people meeting to put on their coats (this is after all England in the summertime!) and walk around the school grounds. The act of stepping outside the building and walking around the footprint of the school site, whether it is in the inner-city or the rural setting, prompts remarkably similar responses. People begin to look at the place which is so familiar to them through another lens. We explore with them the fact that not every day is the same, but there might be a pattern to this day and in paying attention to that pattern we begin to be able to see a different type of school emerging.

The example that I want to provide illustrates a recently held 'walking' enquiry, undertaken in a school in Greater Manchester. It is an old Victorian building, well built in red brick, with solid wooden floors and a lot of interesting old architectural features. Most of the classrooms have windows that are too high to see out of, but the rooms are light and airy, with high ceilings and overall the building itself is well maintained and, considering it is well over one hundred years old, remains a very important part of a very deprived community. The outside of the school is almost entirely made up of tarmac playground, with a high perimeter fence and a small tennis court size garden area which includes a polytunnel and a paved area.

We walked out of school at four pm, just after the students had gone home for the day and we walked slowly around the site.

Place

Enter the playground, what are the colours we see, the smells, the sounds, the textures of this environment? Are they similar as we move around or do we begin to recognize the subtle differences, the shade of the wall which results in a cooler setting, the large red-brick south-facing wall which still radiates the afternoon sunshine or the sitting area near the fence which feels rather harsh and uninviting. We begin to notice the undulation of the site, from the furthest corner of the playground to the top of the playground there is a gentle slope. Is there any sign of any plant life, animal life, birds – or is it entirely child related? What could happen here? We see a potential site for an arena, currently a set of steps, which with a little imagination could serve as a stage. Our agenda is forming, what we see becomes different from what is already present. We begin to share ideas about the spaces, the way that particular plants could be located to grow on the existing boundary and break the monotonous line of municipal green fencing. Our process of enquiry works through an agenda of activities:

Action

Study: What do we see? How does this space currently make sense to us? What does it tell us about how we understand this space as a learning environment?

Create: What could you see? By breaking down the site into a series of different zones, is it possible to construct a learning space which engages with a natural setting?

Techniques: What do we need to adopt to move from what we have to what we might want to have happening on this site?

Concepts: What are the concepts we are trying to establish about the landscape around our school which can be explored through direct intervention with this space?

Enquiry

We spend an hour walking and talking and taking photographs. Then on our return to the staffroom we get a drink and share further. Tasks are administered to investigate further possibilities between now and the next time we meet, to undertake a site assessment to establish some basic information about the infrastructure of services available such as downpipes for grey-water harvesting, potential sites for planting, and potential sources of plants and seedlings. The possibilities of clearing the existing polytunnel of the rubbish and getting it ready for practical use are also investigated.

A couple of weeks later we return to the scene and we reflect on the last occasion when we met. What was surprising? What was unexpected? What was familiar? What was reassuring? Discussion was enthusiastic and engaging, with a considerable amount of excitement about the potential of the use of the space.

We continued to follow a pattern of enquiry:

Choice: What did the set of realistic possibilities look like and what sequence of activity might be followed to achieve them?

Action: Who was going to participate, on what basis? How would this be integrated into the daily activities of the students in the school? What about the involvement of parents and perhaps some supporting local businesses?

Collaboration: Were there other agencies which we could bring into the conversation that could provide specific resources and advice? Which parents were involved in construction, for example, because we wanted to move some heavy concrete slabs and establish a small herb garden which would mean some movement of soil and getting some planters built.

Design: What will this look like? Bringing students and parents into the conversation enhanced the possibility of the site as a working part of the community, where there would be a frequent interplay between learning and production of food for a new community business venture delivering small produce boxes to the neighbourhood with the school as the hub of this activity. New structures, therefore, were needing to be designed; these could be based on existing open-source plans for geodesic domes and polytunnels with relatively little capital outlay. The site begins to be designed as a coherent space, each zone identified according to the microclimate studies that have taken place as well as the water and land space.

Management: How will this operate as a community land resource? What are the governance issues we might need to consider? For example: Are we in a position to establish a community interest company to host and manage the daily activity on the site?

The case notes illustrate how the starting point of simply walking into a space that is familiar and reinventing that space by connecting with the possibilities of what it might become are powerful creative opportunities.

This methodology, which described the way in which a community might explore a set of common interests, is based upon collaborative enquiry, working in teams, meeting, organizing, undertaking activity relevant to the shared interest and then reflecting, coming back with greater insight and awareness. These learning methods are always community minded; they are designed in such a way as to generate association, inspiration and adaptation, as well as to get people to deconstruct the existing circumstance and to look carefully at how it operates, to prompt change, to search for supportive examples, leading to further preparation and checking to ensure that what we are attempting to develop is suited to the context we have uniquely established.

Community-as-action

A particular form of community capability is often found in and around schools in the form of active groups who pursue specific projects on behalf of the school – such as community liaison, parental outreach, after-school and breakfast clubs – all of which illustrate the community function of school.

Community-as-action also illustrates an emergent phenomenon, often generating unexpected and delightfully unpredictable outcomes.

For example: Incredible Edible had a visit from a group of people based in Ghana, West Africa. Two days were spent in the town, during which the visitors spent time talking to different people involved in the project, and they visited a number of the different sites where the project was underway including the town centre, the market, and the schools. On its return to Ghana, the group established its own Incredible Edible project and quickly designed and built a fish farm and a large community growing space at one of the schools. The students were engaged at every point of the food production cycle, from land management and resource utilization, soil management and study, plant nurturing and maintenance, food preparation and cooking, serving and tasting. This community of action has now been taken to the level of adoption into the manifesto for the local political party who wish to establish similar schemes elsewhere. It is also featuring as a part of a Commonwealth of Nations discussion on education for social change and food security and has been presented as a case history for recent international meeting in preparation for the heads of state meeting in Perth later in 2011.

Open source, freedom and change

The final theme of this Exploration focuses upon ways that actions, place, kinship and interest converge upon knowledge. These different dimensions of community serve to both generate and use knowledge and, as part of a knowledge-production resource, we should consider how a sustainable learning community might best profit from the wealth of knowledge for the common good.

My view on this is that we should pursue the idea of open-source sustainability, a way of sharing what we learn through some form of creative common licence, where anyone, anywhere can legitimately gain access to the sum of what we know at any time and be in a position to have access to such knowledge on the simple basis of passing back, when it is appropriate, the learning that they have generated from the use of the ideas. In this way, there is a continuous flow of data from the micro to the macro, enabling specific areas of interest to be pursued and continually informed by the sum of the parts.

In my own recent work, I have experimented with this idea in the form of a website, http://www.school-of-sustainability.com and have established a set of themes based around a Fibonacci spiral which can grow exponentially as more and more material becomes available. Figure 6 is the existing front page of the site, with a set of

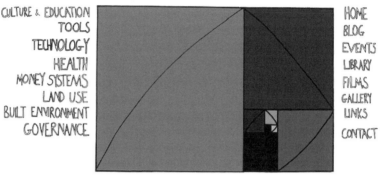

CULTURE & EDUCATION
TOOLS
TECHNOLOGY
HEALTH
MONEY SYSTEMS
LAND USE
BUILT ENVIRONMENT
GOVERNANCE

HOME
BLOG
EVENTS
LIBRARY
FILMS
GALLERY
LINKS
CONTACT

Figure 6 Opening page of http://www.school-of-sustainability.com

themes indicated on the left-hand side, and the resource bank associated with the themes on the right-hand side. The resource is created as an open-source facility, with people posting material as and when they feel it serves a purpose, and users downloading and reporting back on work in progress. As such, it is another version of the school, an open-source school, which can be added to the broader configuration of what we are beginning to see is a new step towards something that will be sustainability led, educational material.

Summary

This Exploration has attempted to provide a stimulus for different ways of thinking about the complicated relationship between school and community. It is often presented as a singular relationship, but there are real and multiple dimensions which have a bearing upon the ways in which understanding can be established and deepened. Instead of suggesting a mechanism that establishes evidence and insight through managerial methods, I have illustrated how a process designed around dialogue and physical engagement with the problem in hand can produce both new and differently conceived results. Approaching established problems in this manner is one way of developing new capabilities that we might need to encourage if we are to truly transform our education system to meet the changing demands of a sustainable society.

It is through a deep and shared consideration of the values that drive and shape our education system that change might be more widely justified or rationalized. When people think about re-visioning education, they often ask 'what kind of young adults do we want to see as a result of this process?' – and those imaginings are shaped by a set of values. At the moment the vision is limited and largely defined by government and extensive and established educational systems; defined – as is the tradition in education – primarily by the values associated with economic productiveness. Perhaps the question needs to shift to 'what kind of sustainable community do we want our schools to build as they redefine their service to others?'

We urgently need the process of learning to be meaningfully integrated into the social, the community context, and for learning transactions (the process of education) to be more closely aligned with the transactions that are necessary for the development of sustainable communities and societies. In the next Exploration we will consider how this might be modelled.

Note

1 See also Clarke (2010a).

Exploration Six
The urban fix: sustainable cities, sustainable minds

Thorough sanitary and remedial action in the houses that we have; and then the building of more, strongly, beautifully, and in groups of limited extent, kept in proportion to their streams and walled round, so that there may be no festering and wretched suburb anywhere, but clean and busy street within and the open country without, with a belt of beautiful garden and orchard round the walls, so that from any part of the city perfectly fresh air and grass and sight of far horizon might be reachable in a few minutes' walk. This is the final aim.

John Ruskin, Sesame and Lillies

I have argued throughout this work that if society is to remediate the situation in which we find ourselves, we need to modify our ways of living and learn a different set of skills that lead to new behaviour and a different future. Part of the big picture we need to comprehend urgently, because civic society depends upon it, is to re-imagine the urban mind and establish the conditions for urban space as a source of sustainable practice, and one such mode of progressing this practice comes through the growing of more of our food in the urban setting. This is needed to establish not only a more sustainable mechanism of food production that does not result in ever-increasing oil miles, but also, and perhaps more importantly, to embed a natural dynamic within the urban space that is the foundation of our learning, the new school, of sustainability. This implies a conceptual break from the consensual view that the urban and the rural are two different environments. They are, in fact, simply differently manipulated settings, in the main manipulated by ourselves for our benefit, and whether the natural environment has a future place remains to be seen.

On face value, the questions raised by the need for food security earlier in this book focus upon the challenge to improve the quality of the environment we find ourselves building in our urban homesteads, to ensure safety of food supply. But the challenge is also perhaps more fundamental; it is to radically rethink the artificiality that comes in a distinction between urban and rural, something we continue to teach our young people and consequently perpetuate as a myth that separates us from understanding our place as part of a natural system. This is a concern that has considerable practical importance. Can we go on thinking that the city is where we do business and the countryside is where we grow the food to feed us? What does that distinction in relationship do to the collective consciousness, particularly in regard to our relationship with life-sustaining eco-systems? (Sterling 2001).

Historically our urban spaces were also food spaces but industrialization changed this. We might ask, 'Is this is now due for a rethink, where we develop from an industrial, linear system, and embed food back into the urban setting?' That is the rationale for what we might call *a school of sustainability* for cities.[1] We could use the idea of a farm (Waters 2008), but not as we know them, to facilitate this; or a store, in the form of a store of knowledge; but it is schools that continue to retain a place of importance in the popular imagination as places of possibility. We expect a lot from our schools as holders of hope for the next generation, so schools of sustainability can become important strategic indicators of both community and societal progress in response to the ecological challenge. Whatever we choose to capture and develop the concepts and resources, it is clear that they will have to be available to all as an inclusive and socially networked facility. They will be ideas for and of the urban space, with connecting technology, open-source sustainability know-how and social networking locked perhaps into the school setting as a feature of urban learning. They become the learning hub for the new urban mind.

Education for eco-urbanism

An awareness of the need to design space for human existence which is comprehensible and not alienating to the general population brings with it a need for clarity and coherence. The clarity comes through the insights that can be drawn from real-time experiences, where people are responding to the ecological challenges they encounter with new and innovative solutions. Urban growing schemes are now a widespread feature of most city landscapes, tucked away on rooftops, stealing a patch on a street corner or a derelict site. As evidence of these small, inventive and imaginatively conceived projects grow, it is becoming clearer that there are recurring patterns of activity that are being adopted by people in different geographical locations. While we are very much in the emergent stages of what might be called a new urban food paradigm, we do not know as yet if all or any of these solutions will work (for example: in generating sufficient food of sufficient quantity to make any substantive contribution to the food security issue). What is clear is that there is a place for capturing, studying and disseminating the new thinking and learning for wider social benefit and adoption, and perhaps the place to connect these practices within a community is school.

If such action were to happen in schools, then what school becomes is a knowledge generating and knowledge using resource, focused on sustainable learning skills, and available as a socially held resource to all. This implies that there needs to be a form of sharing that we learn across diverse and contextually different environments, and utilizing the strengths of human ingenuity and creativity to devise solutions to suit the many places we adopt as our home.

Open-source modelling is the key to this response – a methodology that can capture, study and disseminate the learning. The notion is not particularly new; it is a form of open-source thinking that has been evolving within the information technology community for some considerable time. The transfer of the open-source concept to practical physical activity offers great opportunity for people to mimic and revise existing solutions and gain from earlier models and ideas. This has been a regular feature of the lexicon of designers and urban planners for more than a century (Howard 1902), and more recently has been reconceived in the form of pattern technology (Alexander 1977) and is beginning to show itself in the work of smart cities or eco-cities (Lim and Liu 2010). However, urban planners and architects are not the only engineers of human action, as educators we contribute to the intellectual condition within which new generations entertain how to learn to live in an urban space. As such, we have a role to play in establishing the first principles of an understanding of what it means to live in a sustainable manner.

Part of that engagement as educated citizens comes through the examination of what we mean by quality, particularly the sustainable quality of life that such environments might be able to offer. Simply supplanting an 'eco' prefix to cities is not sufficient to ensure that the lifestyle on offer is capable of meeting the nuances of individual need while ensuring the permanence of the wider system. The smart eco-city that is envisaged recognizes the need for intelligent responses to contemporary environmental challenges, while not ignoring the possibilities of technological advances. It has to be rooted in the practicalities of both ambition and action: to achieve leanness and low-tech thinking, but also to be embedded in the achievable where the methods, tools, and equipment are cheap and easy to access and are suitable for small-scale application but can be accessible across entire systems, and maintain our need for creativity and innovation (Schumacher 1973). A similar approach to education enables learners to engage in curricula which are responsive to identified needs, some of which will be concerned with the carrying capacity of the places where we choose to live.

Perhaps it is easiest to think about this in terms of scale, and again we have a solution embedded directly in our existing communities. To learn to live sustainably, we do not need to think at the scale of a megacity development, nor an entire education system, we think of school. Experience drawn from Incredible Edible suggests we look to the immediate and the practical, at a scale people can personally comprehend and, most importantly, act upon. So, while a backyard, a window ledge, a wall, or a street all become legitimate territory for action, they do not necessarily have the communicative carrying capacity that a centre of education, a school of sustainability might hold. So, extend this one stage further and we begin to consider the public space, the health centre or, indeed, the schoolyard and school base. This has been the locus of change for the Incredible Edible project and many others like it. We start with serious change at the micro-level, we establish them as workable schemes, and we begin to connect them together to form an interdependent technology – a renaissance for the urban mind, a learning hub.

Zero is the measure of our collective action

At the start of this book we asked what is the measure of our collective actions? Whereas we have grown accustomed to the metric of large-scale as a good (in the form of growth, progress and development in scale and size), our new defining characteristics of success might better be thought of, in the light of what we have considered here, as being the achievement of zero. So, to aim for zero:

- zero carbon
- zero waste
- zero growth (if that growth means the exploitation of the finite planetary resources)
- zero environmental impact, or indeed zero plus in that we begin to enhance and improve upon earlier circumstances
- zero forced extinctions
- zero climate damage
- zero soil degradation

- zero pollution
- zero net greenhouse gas emissions
- zero encroachment on nature.

We begin to fashion the schema of our new metric, which in turn enables us to report in a new way the success of our school systems. How to establish new ways of thinking and understanding the cityscapes we increasingly find ourselves living in as zero environments is therefore of great interest, as clearly our existing solutions are failing to rectify past, growth-focused failure.

When we talk of eco-cities and smart cities, we run the danger of revisiting the utopian dreams of yester-year, where the old idea of master-plans for cities generated what Mark Jazombek (2010) calls an 'illusion' of the city: 'A place where social and economic problems and politics have all been photo-shopped away.' The danger of the master plan is the elimination of the day-to-day realities. The great advantage of the micro-change approach is that the day-to-day realities are the drawing board for contact and connection, they define the sustainability contextually. Instead of establishing conditions for sustainability, we use these micro-plans that arise from urban growing projects, with all of their nuanced and sensitive solutions to the small locales they operate within, as the foundations of an eco-revolution. This is the real-politik as it is based upon existing failed infrastructure, failed political alliances, undocumented citizens, and short-term, greenscape fixes. That is why, from an educational perspective, we must begin in the places we currently use: our schoolyards, our public spaces, our health centres, parks and derelict sites. There is vast potential for revision and experimentation, but it has to form into something of overarching purpose, and this is where the focus on food provides a significant opportunity for new thinking.

What happens in those places is becoming a movement of people reclaiming the city for themselves. They are generating the data sets for our new urban learning hubs, the fertile growing spaces created in schoolyards are an extension of just such schemes. What may look like an innocent raised bed is actually the representation of a radical realignment of human thinking about the urban space as the knowledge of how, why and where emerges.

School of sustainability

In our schools which are exploring the numerous ways in which they can use their schoolyards as part of an open-source sustainability concept, we begin to see the possibilities of the zero option where a pattern of activity leads to measurable effects and deeper insights against critical sustainability themes. Our interest is not on the growing of a few vegetables but, instead, on the ways in which the focus on growing food can stimulate a whole set of relationships across a school site to inform and guide community learning about urban sustainability. The more we have done this, the more we begin to understand that the marginal activity, such as a vegetable or flower bed, can not only function below the policy radar, but can also be used as a Trojan horse to establish a starting point of action through which people can begin to think and act radically through education for the world we occupy. This is a foundation to influence the world we might be moving towards.

In the case of Incredible Edible for example, we have already seen how this has extended across an entire community. Our interest was a change in the social behaviour, and a challenge to the practical choices we make as we go about daily life. As yet, this work remains in the early stages of development, but important pointers are nevertheless emerging about how to facilitate change.

Instead of a master plan, there are a multitude of micro-projects underway (from backyard eggs, to hydroponics, bread making, orchard planting, cheese making, plant growing and bee-keeping) which can be examined in terms of yield potential, soil fertility and management sciences, uses of vertical growing spaces, design and development of micro-schemes for walls and rooftops, water capture processes, passive solar gain projects – all serving as templates for providing people with the types of solutions that they require. In particular, they challenge the myth of sustainability and that industrialized view of nature and people not mixing. In growing in the urban space and establishing a new paradigm for that growing, and including learning as a central feature of the work in progress, we begin to see the prospect of a new form of urban life, based around day-to-day capabilities, not some utopian design but a curriculum for life and of life.

By taking the environmentalism out of the urban mix, the experimental projects are starting to get beyond the implausibility of 'nature as happy, green and friendly', to a simple practical relationship of convenience that takes us out of the predictable frameworks through the integration of urban and rural by bringing a new form of learning to the townscape.[2] It has to be noted that this also has little to do with generating 'local' produce, which perpetuates a particular form of market-trading promoting elite foods distinct from all other foods. Instead, by growing food inside city space experiments with the urban idea, it represents a way of responding to the food security crisis; first symbolically and, perhaps at a later stage, as an embedded feature of the urban landscape and mindscape. That is why the potential gains of using schoolyards as the new urban farm are so attractive, because they connect a number of important elements. School is a point of contact for a community of people for many reasons. There is a shared interest in making the learning context real, provocative and purposeful for the participants involved; there is great interest in how we might ensure that school has relevance to young people; and the existing fragmentation of enterprise and education can be overcome as the produce arising from the schemes can be developed commercially, thereby enabling further projects to be self-funded rather than externally-funded.

So, the school of sustainability is not a school at all in the traditional sense. Instead it represents the attitude of sustainability in practice, a way of providing a design through which community food security can begin to become a feature of a new curriculum for urban life – a curriculum that sees growing, and experimentation of growing, in the urban setting as part of a vast, urban open-source programme – a fix for the unsustainable urban mind.

Summary

In his Reith Lectures of 1995, 'Cities for a small planet', Richard Rogers (1997) presented some startling data that illustrated the effect that the car had made to the urban designed space. 'An efficient parking standard requires twenty square metres for a single car. Even supposing that only one in five inhabitants owns a car, then a city of ten million (i.e. London) needs an area about ten times the size of the City of London just to park cars.' The streets, corners, design of everything from signage to lampposts are all driven by the needs of the motorist. It is an interesting observation of the way that our small choices dictate how we live. In a recent publicity project, we drew attention to the space the car takes by 'renting' a car parking space for an entire day and laying a vegetable patch, complete with plants on the parking bay of a city high street. The resulting interest from the people who passed by was startling. Quite what such actions lead to we do not know. However, it helps people to imagine what a city might look like if there were no cars. Radicalizing the urban mind is not difficult, it is examples people need and once they get them they do the rest themselves.

So a new space emerges, and into that space emerge new opportunities. Such is the present issue with schools and sustainable education – a glimmer of possibility lies ahead as we reconsider the appropriateness of the school for the ecological age. It is as significant a moment as that which began compulsory schooling more than 150 years ago, a moment when we can imagine again the 'Scale – planetary, Scope – centuries, and Stakes – civilization' needs for the twenty-first century, and take a risk.

Ruskin's imaginative leap to the garden city was formed at a time before the pervasive effect of the car, and it served to inform a view of ourselves and nature that has persisted until now. It is time for us to step beyond that romanticized industrial mind, to put industrialism away and to see cities as our new natural places, and use that as the basis of a practical food-inspired revolution. That revolution will begin to redefine the artifice of natural and urban. Through that redefinition we might be able to see what the new urban mind could become. That is the final story in this book, how we undertake our great work.

Notes

1 For a more extensive discussion of the issues related to this please refer to my website http://www.school-of-sustainability.com where there is also an extensive bibliography.
2 See Berry 1999, Lovelock 2009 and an extensive commentary by McIntosh 2008.

Exploration Seven
Our great work: education for sustainability

> *You cannot carry out fundamental change without a certain amount of madness. In this case, it comes from nonconformity, the courage to turn your back on the old formulas, the courage to invent the future. It took the madmen of yesterday for us to be able to act with extreme clarity today. I want to be one of those madmen. We must dare to invent the future.*
>
> Thomas Sankara (1985: 141–4)

Thomas Berry wrote some magnificent books. In one of them, *The Great Work*, he observed the following: there are occasions in human history when we look back with the luxury of time and we recognize that the choices people were making at a given moment were setting the future course of history. While the specific moments were not heralded, the cumulative impact of human activity cannot be underestimated. There were moments when great visionaries lived, and they presented to the people of the world a view that transcended their own time and put us in the context of the universal, a longitudinal time-frame of human history. We can reflect on the many prophets, gurus and spiritual leaders, we can think of the musicians, artists and storytellers, our Michelangelos and Leornardo Da Vincis of the West. We can also think of the specific historians, people such as Ssu-ma Ch'ien in China, Ibn Khaldun in the Arab world and the Greek Thucydides. All of these in their own ways represent breakthroughs in the human journey, each taking us to a higher level of awareness and consciousness.

Berry observed that the sum of these contributions across the divide of time created great civilizations, cultures and dynasties. They were instrumental in assembling ways of governing the individual and collective mind to connect the sacred with the practical; they were formative elements in generating the basic norms of reality through which people designed their lives. A deeply connected thread across these varying nations and realities has been the fact that in the main, for many thousands of years, human beings have lived a relatively sublime existence in keeping with natural systems; and in so doing they sustained a quality of life that connected directly with nature.

These civilizations of our shared human past were sophisticated and cultured, and they were founded on a practical understanding of the connection between spirit and nature that was often witnessed in their temples, cathedrals and sacred places. It was through an eco-literate agrarian consciousness (Denton-Thompson 2009) that this connection between the human and the planet, the nature and the spirit, the self and universal was demonstrated and maintained. However, despite the immense legacy they represent, on their own they no longer provide us with enough guidance. The lessons they give us of the past are insufficient to guide us into the future, because our intervention in the world is so significantly different now from that past record. We cannot function without these lessons, but they are insufficient in themselves to generate a collective critique of the way we now live our lives in post-industrial and post-production society. We are out of step with ourselves and with our world upon which we depend. Something is happening that is profoundly different – apart from the lessons we have learned from the past, we need to form the conditions to enable a new vision for the future to emerge.

The ecological significance of *now*

In this book I have suggested that it is important to re-imagine our place and our moment in the face of time. We have to rethink how we establish our urban space, and one way to achieve this is to transform education from an instrument of industrial consciousness, to an instrument of ecological consciousness. I have suggested that the evidence is clearly in front of us that the environmental crisis is a fact of our time and this alone distances us from our fellow human beings of the past.[1] The human effect on planet earth is now sufficiently damaging to suggest we need to consider a change in the way we are living. As Rees (2003: 2) observes:

> We still live, as all our ancestors have done, under the threat of disasters that could cause worldwide devastation: volcanic super-eruptions and major asteroid impacts, for instance. Natural catastrophes on this global scale are fortunately so infrequent, and therefore unlikely to occur within our own lifetime, that they do

not preoccupy our thoughts, nor give most of us sleepless nights. But such catastrophes are now augmented by other environmental risks that we are bringing upon ourselves, risks that cannot be dismissed as improbable.

Our presence here on earth is no longer benign; we are no longer 'one species among many'. Instead, we are a dominant species exerting that dominance over all other forms of life. This is a different relationship to that of our ancestors, it is now the case that everything else depends upon how we decide to survive. We enter a new ethical time.

This change is historically significant, brought about by disturbing the biosphere to such an extent through human industrial actions that we are now at an impasse in our relationship with the earth. It has no parallel in historical terms of ecological shift since the geobiological transitions that occurred some 65 million years ago. At that time, history witnessed the passing of the dinosaurs and a new biological age began. This was the lyric-age of life on earth, and so it has been until now. Evidence from all corners of the planet suggests that, through our wanton destruction of the natural environment, there is a profound change taking place globally. This change is likely to take centuries for our species to respond and adapt, if we are able to do so at all.[2]

Perception of now

The questions that these challenges raise are legion, but ultimately converge upon a simple matter of response. Do we bury our heads in the sand, live in denial and proceed as usual? Do we worry, but think we cannot do anything? Do think of this as a period for creative innovation and opportunity? Do we see it as a period when we should legislate and restrict human impact as best we can?

If we can begin to understand our identity in relation to other living things, we begin to recognize we are all part of a great story and that we each play a part in its narrative. Education is our route-way to this position. This narrative takes us from the distorted reality of the industrialized world towards the 'deep ecology' that Arne Naess (1988) introduced to refer to the implicit penetration of ecology into all other fields of study, including the human condition itself. Starting this process of change and re-alignment of the human race with the planet, we will change our behaviour; in effect we will act upon enlightened self-interest for personal survival. Already it is clear that enough people, in enough parts of the world, recognize this and they represent a poignant political impetus for change.

What is happening now, in the multivarious communities engaged in micro-activity across the world, is an awakening and a response to the fact that our human centric relationship with the planet is causing too much damage, and the resulting actions are geared towards changing that relationship to make it more earth centric in keeping with the needs of the natural environment. These actions will have implications for every citizen, as it will become ever more likely that governments will demand personal changes to urban lifestyles, just as much as they will mandate further for regulation on carbon emissions and energy useage by industry. These represent formative changes in what is highly likely to be a much longer-term global effort, one that in future times may be seen as just as significant as those moments of our shared past that changed the course of our life on earth. It is hoped that the next few years will set the conditions for generations to come to be able to live fulfilling lives, while at the same time ensuring that they have the necessary knowledge and conscious awareness of what we do and why we do it. That is why what we do now, and how we learn to do new things at the community level, is so important in setting the tone of change for our urban life. Furthermore, and because this involves learning something new, the demands that will be placed upon education will be greater than ever before. In effect we have to rise to the challenge of this time, to paraphrase Thomas Berry – we have to do our Great Work. We have to educate for sustainability, for now and forever. It is as simple and as complex as that.

This book has emerged from my work with schools and communities over the past two decades. During this time I have observed the schools in those communities grappling with a constant barrage of reform. While the reform might have come from central government of a singular political persuasion, it has singularly failed, as with previous efforts, to demonstrate any coherent and consistent philosophy of education, nurture and learning for sustainable living.

Instead, experience tells me that educational reform is fragmented, piecemeal, arbitrary, and regularly linked to the opportunistic whims of ministers who have parliamentary careers in mind far more than educational enrichment. They move on to other jobs with alarming speed, suggesting that the education brief is only a short-term tenure and leaving their legacy in classrooms across the country in the form of half-baked schemes and programmes which collide with their previous incumbent's ideas. Educational reform has, for many, managed to generate a climate where people on the front-line, teachers and students, feel exploited, undervalued, manipulated by management and bullied into fitting into a system that they often report as being out of step with both the students that they work with, and without any core philosophy or any compelling vision of the present, let alone the future.

We seem to have created little more than an educational wilderness, whereas Jones (2008) says:

> We have communities with nothing in common, where individualism is so embedded and institutionalized that it has eroded any semblance of policy of care, idealism, or commitment to each other, and this is eating away at the true values of service, interdependence and relationships, the stuff that builds resilient communities, the stuff that helps us to take the really big risks of transforming our living places so they in turn can transform lives.

As a result of this set of circumstances conspiring against school, we turn to community; the climate is muddied even further by diverse and contradictory perspectives on the purpose of schools within their many and varied communities. It is true to say that there remains a resilient faith in human-scale practices in many individual school communities and the places they serve. Scratch the surface of the normally functioning, compliant school and in many cases you quickly recognize schools are full of inquisitive people managing a vibrant internal conversation about living, connection, creativity and possibility – a similar picture exists outside the school gate. My suggestion is that these places manage this despite, and not because of, the prevailing externally defined conditions and parameters of performance and community expectation. In effect, their internal culture is a counter-culture, functioning for the purpose of maintenance of what the school defines as its own ethos but, perhaps more poignantly, representing a form of resistance and protest to the prevailing order that can transcend the school and become a call for something different.

There is therefore something slightly adrift in this post-industrial period. We are living through what commentators such as Vaclev Havel describe as a 'period of turbulence'. That is, a time when a lot of things seem to be blurred at the edges and previous certainties are not quite as certain as they once were. The idea of 'school', and the whole school system from cradle to grave, is clearly changing, as expectations of what schools do and how they do it are modified by the socio-cultural context in which they function. Whereas, even a decade ago, we could look across the school system and see a consistent pattern of organization and structure, we now see a plethora of different school models which have generated new and different configurations of relationships between students, parents, teachers, governors, local authorities and government.

On the one hand, these restructurings represent something of the state of the nation and the consequence of the economic zeitgeist of individualism and choice. On the other, they indicate a singular lack of clarity about the nature and purpose of school. While diversity of practice may in many ways be desirable, a sense of consistency in the quality of provision is now needed, but the defining features of that quality are not as yet formulated, and the opportunity is therefore present for something radically new to be positioned in the debate.

Out of all this complex mix, there remains a common denominator at play – schooling. Underneath all of the reform, there remains a fundamental commitment to the idea that school, as an institution, is not questioned, and that its function by and large remains intact despite the contextual changes happening beyond the school gates. We might have many versions of school available, from Trusts to Academies, Charter to Free schools, but the truth is that the core technology remains fundamentally the same.

The point I have tried to make in this book is that a new role and function in the form of the school of sustainability is already present around us. Such a school is one that lies at the heart of its community as a hub for a connection of the urban and the rural, a connection of the mindscape with the landscape. This school is focused in my view through the science, art, technology and craft of living sustainably, but it is not as yet formalized as an institution, it is instead the emergent action of people looking for the next way to live in the urban space. That is the starting point for a transformation of the school into a centrepiece of a community that is working on a route-way to a more resilient, connected future.

To get there, we draw upon existing examples and models. It will be a turbulent journey, as the old definitions of school die hard. Pearce (1998) calls the unfailing commitment to the idea of school, a 'radical denial'. Our denial is pathological, and attends to treating the failure of small elements in the belief that the system is intact, rather than asking about the system as a whole and its continual need for attention being demonstrable evidence of failure at a much wider level. We have what the fourteenth-century Spanish Sufi, Ibn Arabi, called 'our enormous capacity for self-deception' managing our collective desire collectively to maintain things as they are and to carefully modify them, and yet what we have may not be correctable.

I hold a similar view to that of Pearce. My suggestion in this book has been to look again at what we are doing. When a system is completely out of alignment with the world it is meant to connect with, it is not enough to simply play with the existing arrangements and hope they will reconnect. An immediate response might be to find and then introduce a new approach that is more productive, and to eradicate the earlier approach and start to think about what we might want to do next. However, this instrumental approach is not really productive and it is not what I think will happen. Instead, I think we are better served thinking about the system and how a system changes. What I continue to explore in the many and varied discussions that have surrounded these ideas are elements of a larger whole; what we will find is that things which attract each other have the potential to generate a new coherence. We don't need to orchestrate a transition, it will come anyway (Senge *et al.* 2004); we need to understand what those transitional material processes look like – this is what I have described as sustainable pattern and it informs my work in the School-of-Sustainability forum.

As the prologue to the World Expo in 2000 (The Hannover Principles) said:

> Human society needs to aspire to an integration of its material, spiritual and ecological elements. Current technologies, processes and means tend to separate these facets rather than connect them. Nature uses the sun's energy to create interdependent systems in which complexity and diversity imply sustainability. In contrast, industrialized society extracts energy for systems designed to reduce natural complexity. The challenge for humanity is to develop human design processes which enable us to remain in the natural context. Almost every phase of the design, manufacturing, and construction processes requires reconsideration. Linear systems of thought, or short-term programs which justify ignorant, indifferent, or arrogant means are not farsighted enough to serve the future of the interaction between humanity and nature. We must employ both current knowledge and ancient wisdom in our efforts to conceive and realize the physical transformation, care and maintenance of the Earth.
>
> Hannover Principles 2000

The need to reconnect, redesign and realign our actions generates a series of challenges concerning the relationship with self, organization and systems, raises questions. How might we best move forward, from where we are, to something else? The idea of deterministic change never appealed to me, and two decades of educational reform proves one thing if nothing else: that what you want is not what you get if you adopt the political view that reform can be mandated. So there seems to be something to learn methodologically about reform that might be valuable to capture and address within a conversation about 'present and future' school. Equally, there is something about the idea of the concept of the concept of school and the reality of school. By this I mean the concept of learning things, building upon existing knowledge and using this in productive ways as a resource through which we can develop, both personally and as a civilization. At the same time, where this happens, the locus of learning is clearly no longer locked to any one place. So schooling is at once local and universal. We need, I think, to explore this idea much further and this book has simply started the conversation through the explorations described.

So, at the end of this book, I have arrived at the starting point for the next phase of my work. The work seeks to establish a series of connections; the way we might connect with each other, with our world and with our cherished institutions.

While we all work out our daily lives on the general and the practical level, I think there are ways of taking the principles of sustainability further. Establishing a more progressive idea of sustainability helps us to step beyond the first stage, a view of some ways of living sustainably, and radically challenges all that exists in the fabric of the human society to be realigned to progressive sustainable principles. The zero metric, as absurd as it may seem, generates a direction of travel which may in time prove to be our survival route. This work has tried to provide something of an outline sketch of what sustainable education and a school of sustainability might be, but does so with a health warning – we do not really know as yet, and we need to begin to create, the body of knowledge to guide and inform our judgement. What we do know is that nature is there to guide and, regardless of what happens to us, will continue to be there. I recognize the immensity of the work ahead. The pattern which I sketched is the first attempt at a device that can provide a way of exploring many of these ideas with colleagues. However, it may be enough for the moment to simply suggest that, in achieving a goal of creating a sustainable learning community, we have to succeed beyond, between and within our existing idea of school:

Beyond

- *Holistic* – We acknowledge that we educate the whole person; education nourishes our sources of collective wealth – environmental, human, social, spiritual, manufactured and financial.
- *Ethical* – We educate to ensure that we extend our care and our concerns beyond the present and into the future.

- *Innovative* – We educate in the confidence that our personal and collective efforts will seek to integrate and generate new insights.
- *Equitable* – We educate with an awareness that resources are finite, and that we have a duty of care for each other and for the planet.

Between

- *Connected* – We educate to help us to see the relational patterns that inform change, from local to global, from individual to group, from living being to planet, from past to present to future, from micro to macro, from collective to self, from real to virtual.
- *Systemic* – We educate to see the dynamics of systems, of seasons, of the interrelatedness of ecology, of the interdependence of one system upon and within another.
- *Contextualized* – We educate to recognize the place we play in our own environment, and how we influence our surroundings by the choices we make.
- *Critical* – We educate to help us not to take the world as given; instead we develop the capability to enquire, deconstruct, confront and reconstruct.

Within

- *Emerging* – We educate to construct an operational approach to organization which is generative and is deeply aware of the possibility of change.
- *Living systems* – We educate to illustrate and understand how we are part of a wider, integrated living system, and that we naturally move through phases of renewal, development, conservation and creative destruction both personally and collectively in our relationships with each other and with the planet.
- *Process* – We educate with a deep appreciation of process as a way of constructing meaning and establishing pedagogy, everyone is a learner, reflective practice is our core methodology, our learning is participatory and grounded.
- *Natural* – We use nature as both teacher and guide, and we take every opportunity to connect our learning to natural examples and illustrations.
- *Freedom* – We educate to ensure that every person understands and celebrates freedom; this is exemplified through choice, learning styles, learning methods, and is grounded in dialogue, participation and community.

- *Interdependence* – We educate to see the fundamental of interdependence – we all rely upon each other and we all rely upon our planetary environment for survival.
- *Creativity* – We educate to encourage and nurture the innate creative potential of every person viewing the realization of creative potential as a fundamental human right rather than an elitist or marginal pursuit.

This, I think, sets a scene for the work. It is work which will scope one way forward with the venture of education for sustainable living, and in turn a new idea of school for sustainability. I hope it will begin to illustrate in more meaningful and connected ways what communites might aspire towards when they grapple with the challenge to become sustainable. It is one way forward, it is deliberate in:

- being idealistic
- being committal
- seeking forms of interdependence
- seeking pattern and coherence
- recognizing difference but understanding that there are mutually held needs
- open for all, an open-source sustainability.

The formulation of sustainable learning communities has to become the quest for our own renaissance and harmony with the world we inhabit. As I have reported, there is a connection between the imaginative and the physical reality of our world, and this relationship changes all the time. Pearce (2002: 15) observes:

> Metanoia restructures, to varying degrees and even for varying lengths of time, those basic representations of reality inherited from the past. On those representations we base our notions or concepts of what is real. In turn, our notions of what is real direct our perceptual apparatus, that network of senses that tells us what we feel, hear, see, and so on. This is not a simple subjective manoeuvre, but a reality-shaping procedure.

If we believe that reality is just 'out there', and what is 'within' us is simply a perceptual jotting-pad noting the activity of the world as it travels past us, then our engagement with the world is utterly fatalistic, disengaged and rudderless. It fails to connect the hand to the earth, heart to heart, and mind to mind. If we simply see what we see and don't connect with our inner-self, two things seem to happen. We end up receiving the world as victims rather than a part of a fragile and sensitive infrastructure of ecosystems, both physically and psychically real; and we fall victim to seeing the world in the way we are taught to see it, and because we are disengaged onlookers we treat physical reality as yet another commodity.

But we don't have to approach daily reality like this and accept it for what it might appear to be. As Schumacher says in his concluding section of *Small is Beautiful* (1993: 252):

> Everywhere people ask: What can I actually do? The answer is as simple as it is disconcerting; we can, each of us, work to put our own house in order. The guidance we need for this work cannot be found in science or technology, the value of which utterly depends on the ends they serve; but it can still be found in the traditional wisdom of mankind.

The importance of the need to deepen our collective understanding of a new realism of mind couldn't be greater than in our present time. We need to see our relationship to each other, and to the world we live in and depend upon, as a foundation for our actions. This is not a silent protest, but a careful connection outwards to each other and each living thing. Instead of denying the presence and significance of the outer environment that nourishes and maintains life, we need to rebuild our connection to it. In finding that connection, we also delve far more deeply into our inner self. We might rediscover what, for many, is denied and disregarded as being of any value, a spiritual self – what for so many is now a shadow-being. However, that is a whole other work, another part of the rich tapestry we might just weave together as we move forward.

Notes

1 For a more extensive discussions of the issues related to this, please refer to my website http://www.school-of-sustainability.com where there is also an extensive bibliography.
2 See Berry 1999, Lovelock 2009, and an extensive commentary by McIntosh 2008.
3 Senge *et al.* (2004).

References

Agenda 21: 'The Earth Summit strategy to save our planet', Boulder, CO: Earth Press.

Alexander, C. (1977) *A Pattern Language*. Oxford: Oxford University Press.

Alexander, C., Ishikawa, S., Silverstein, M., with Jacobson, M., Fiksdahl-King, I. and Angel, S. (1977) *A Pattern Language*. New York: Oxford University Press.

Allison, I. (2009) 'The Copenhagen Diagnosis: Updating the World on the Latest Climate Science', UNSW Climate Change Research Center, Sydney, Australia, p. 11.

Arnold, Matthew (1994) *Culture and Anarchy*. Yale: New Haven.

Atkinson, T. and Claxton, G. (eds) (2000) *The Intuitive Practitioner*. Buckingham: Open University Press.

Aune, J. (2009) 'Only connect, between morality and ethics in Habermas' communication theory', *Communication Theory* 17(4): 340–347.

Barth, M., Godemann, J., Rieckmann, M. and Stoltenberg, U. (2007) 'Developing key competencies for sustainable development in higher education', *International Journal of Sustainability in Higher Education* 8(4): 416–430.

Beddington, J. (2009) 'World faces perfect storm of environmental problems by 2030', *Guardian*, 18th March 2009.

Benus, J. M. (2008) 'Nature's 100 best: Top biomimicry solutions to environmental crisies', Bioneers 19th Annual Conference. San Rafael, CA. 19th October 2008, plenary address.

Berry, T. (1999) *The Great Work – Our Way into the Future*. New York: Crown Publishing.

Berry, T. (2005) Personal correspondence.

Berry, T. (2009) *The Sacred Universe. Earth, spirituality and religion in the 21st century*. New York: Bell Tower.

Binney, G. and Williams, C. (1995) *Leaning into the Future*. London: Nicholas Brealey Publishing.

Birney, A. and Reed, J. (2009) *Sustainability and Renewal: Findings from the leading sustainable schools research project*. Nottingham: NCSL.

Birol, F. (2008) *World Energy Outlook*. Paris: International Energy Agency.

Bohm, D. (1996) *On Dialogue*. London: Routledge.

Brand, S. (2009) *Whole Earth Discipline*. London: Viking–Penguin Books.

Braungart, M. and McDonough, W. (2002) *Cradle to Cradle. Remaking the way we make things*. New York: North Point Press. (Note: Walter Stahel is recognized as being the originator of the term Cradle to Cradle some 25 years ago; this has subsequently been taken up in the work of Braungart and McDonough (2002 onwards).)

Brown, L. (2002) *Eco-economy. Building an economy for the earth*. Washington: Earth policy Institute.

Brown, L. R. (2003) *Plan B: Rescuing a planet under stress and a civilisation in trouble*. New York: W.W. Norton & Company.

Capra, F. (2005) 'Preface', in M. Stone and Z. Barlow (eds), *Ecological Literacy: Educating our children for a sustainable world*. San Francisco: Sierra Books.

Carson, R. (1962) *Silent Spring*. New York: Fawcett Crest.

Chomsky, N. (2006) *Failed States: The abuse of power and the assault on democracy*. London: Penguin Books.

Clarke, P. (2000) *Learning Schools, Learning Systems*. London: Continuum.

Clarke, P. (2005) *Improving Schools in Difficulty* (Improving Schools Series). London: Continuum.

Clarke, P. (2008) 'Sustainable Education'. *Professional Development Today* 11(3): 18–21.

Clarke, P. (2008) 'Using an established school improvement program to build capacity at school and system level: IQEA The Hong Kong Programme', in John Chi-ken Lee and Ling-po Shiu (eds), *Developing Teachers and Developing Schools in Changing Contexts*. Hong Kong: Chinese University Press, pp. 315–336.

Clarke, P. (2009a) *Incredible Edible: Growing Community*. Todmorden: IET Publications.

Clarke, P. (2009b) 'A practical guide to radical transition: framing the sustainable community', *Education, Knowledge and Economy* 3(3): 183–197.

Clarke, P. (2009c) 'Sustainability and Improvement: A problem "of" education and "for" education', *Improving Schools* 12(1): 11–17.

Clarke, P. (2010a) 'Community renaissance', in M. Coates (ed.), *Shaping a New Educational Landscape*. London: Continuum.

Clarke, P. (2010b) 'Incredible Edible: how to grow sustainable communities', *Forum* 52(1): 69–79.

Clarke, P. (2010c) 'Paper title: Tiny worlds and big realities – creating sustainable communities in the Google-age'. Keynote presentation at the Perstalozzi Programme: Council of Europe Bergen, Norway 14/09/2010–17/09/2010.

Clarke, P. (2011) 'Cultivating a future'. Keynote presentation at the 24th International School Effectiveness and Improvement Congress, Limassol Cyprus 3rd–7th January 2011.

Cohen, M. (1993) 'Integrated ecology: the process of counseling with nature', *The Humanist Psychologist* 21(3).

Commonwealth of Australia (2009) 'Living sustainably: The Australian Government's National Action Plan for Education for Sustainability (2009)', Environment Standards Branch Department of the Environment, Water, Heritage and the Arts GPO Box 787 Canberra ACT 2601.

De Guimps, R. (1904) *Pestalozzi, His Life and Works*. New York: Appleton and Company.

Denton-Thompson, M. (2009) Private correspondence.

Esbjorn-Hargens, S. and Zimmerman, M. E. (2009) *Integral Ecology – Using multiple perspectives on the natural world*. Boston, MA: Integral Books.

Finger, M. and Asún, J. M. (2001) *Adult Education at the Crossroads. Learning our way out*, London: Zed Books.

Flannery, T. (2007) Source: http://www.meteogroup.co.uk/uk/home/weather/weather-news/news/ch/afa684518e6bfe8495fbaa763d860b40/article/climate_change-3.html (last accessed December 10th 2009).

Freire, P. (1992) *A Pedagogy of Hope*. Chippenham: Continuum Publishing.

Fullan, M. (1993) *The New Meaning of Educational Change*. London: Cassell.

Gajardo, M (1994) 'Ivan Illich', in Z. Morsy (ed.) *Key Thinkers in Education Volume 2*, Paris: UNESCO Publishing.

Goleman, D. (2009) *Ecological Intelligence*. New York: Broadway Books.

Grahn, P., Martensson, F., Lindblad, B., Nilsson, P. and Ekman, A. (1997) *Ute på Dagis Stad and Land 145*. Håssleholm, Sweden: Nora Skåne Offset.

Gribbin, J. (2004) *Deep Simplicity. Chaos, complexity and the emergence of life*. London: Penguin.

Hegerl, G. C. (1996) 'Detecting Greenhouse-Gas-Induced Climate Change with an Optimal Fingerprint Method', *Journal of Climate*, 9(October): 2281–2306.

Hobsbawm, E. (2009) 'Socialism has failed. Now capitalism is bankrupt. So what comes next?' *Guardian*, 10th April 2009, p. 33.

Holmberg, J. and Samuelsson, B. E. (eds) (2006) 'Drivers and barriers for implementing sustainable development in Higher Education.' Göteborg Workshop, December 7–9, 2005. UNESCO, Education for Sustainable Development in Action, Technical Paper No. 3, September 2006.

Holzer, S. (2010) *Permaculture*. East Meon: Permanent Publications.

Hopkins, D., Ainscow, M. and West, M. (1996) *Improving the Quality of Education for All*. London: David Fulton Publishing.

Hopkins, R. (2008) *The Transition Handbook*. Dartington: Green Books.

Howard, E. (1902) *Garden Cities of Tomorrow*. London: Sonnenschein & Co.

HRH Prince of Wales, Jupiter, T. and Skelly, I. (2010) *Harmony: A New Way of Looking at Our World*. London: Blue Door.

Hundertwasser (2006) *Hundertwasser Architecture*. London: Taschen.

Hungerford, H. and Volk, T. (1990) 'Changing learner behavior through environmental education', *Journal of Environmental Education* 21(3): 8–21.

Hussain, W. (2009) 'Gross national happiness in Bhutan: A living example of an alternative approach to progress'. Wharton International Research Experience. University of Pennsylvania.

Illich, Ivan (1973) *Tools for Conviviality*. London: Open Books.

Illich, Ivan (1975) *Medical Nemesis: The expropriation of health*, London: Marian Boyars.

Illich, Ivan and Verne, E. (1976) *Imprisoned in the Global Classroom*, London: Writers and Readers Publishing Co-operative.

IPCC (2004) '4th Annual Assessment Report, Summary for Policymakers'. Paris: International Panel for Climate Change.

Jackson, T. (2009) *Prosperity Without Growth. Economics for a finite planet*. London: Earthscan.

Jarzombek, M. (2010) 'Post–sustainability', in C.J Lim and E. Liu (2010) *Smart Cities and Eco Warriors*. London: Routledge.

Jickling, B. (1992). 'Why I don't want my children to be educated for sustainable development', *Journal of Environmental Education* 23(4): 5–8.

Jones, T. (2007) *Utopian Dreams*. London: Faber and Faber.

Kellstedt, P. M., Zahran, S. and Vedlitz, A. (2008) 'Personal efficacy, the information environment, and attitudes toward global warming and climate change in the United States', *Risk Analysis* 28(1): 113–126.

Kelly, A. (2009) 'Education futures and schooling theory: Adapting Sen's early work on capability to choice and sustainability'. Personal correspondence.

Kelly, A. (2010) Personal correspondence.

Kirschenmann, F. L. (2010) *Cultivating and Ecological Conscience*. Lexington, KY: University Press of Kentucky.

Klein, N. (2001) *No Logo*. London: Flamingo.

Kumar, S. (2002) *You are therefore I am: A declaration of dependence*. Dartington: Green Books Ltd.

Laszlo, K. (2001) 'The evolution of Business: Learning, Innovation and Sustainability in the 21st century'. Paper presented at the 45th Annual Conference of The International Society for the Systems Sciences (ISSS) Asilomar, California. July 2001.

Leadbeater, C. (2000) *Living on Thin Air. The new economy*, London: Penguin.

Lim, C. J and Liu, E. (2010) *Smart Cities and Eco Warriors*. London: Routledge.

Lloyds of London (2010) *360 Degree Insights. Globalisation and environment*. London: Lloyds.

Lovelock, J. (2006) *The Revenge of Gaia*. London: Allen Lane.

Lovelock, J. (2009) *The Vanishing Face of Gaia*. London: Allen Lane.

McIntosh, A. (2001) *Soil and SOUL*. London: Aurum Press.

McIntosh, A. (2008) *Hell and High Water*. Edinburgh: Berlin Limited.

McIntosh, A. (2008) 'Rekindling Community: Connecting people, environment and spirituality', *Schumacher Briefings 15*. Bristol: Green Books.

McKeown, R. (2002). *Education for Sustainable Development Toolkit, Version 2*, Energy. Knoxville, TN: Environment and Resources Center, University of Tennessee, pp. 12–13.

Macy, J. and Young Brown, M. (1998) *Coming Back to Life: Practices to Reconnect Our Lives, Our World*. Gabriola Island, BC: New Society Publishers.

Monbiot, G. (2001) *Captive State. The corporate takeover of Britain*, London: Pan.

Naess, A. (1988) 'Deep ecology and ultimate premises', *Ecologist* 18: 128–131.

National Medium and Long-term Talent Development Plan (2010–2020) People's Republic of China. Source http://www.brookings.edu/papers/2010/ 1123_china_talent_wang.aspx (last accessed on 14/12/2010).

National Research Council (NRC) (2006) *Surface Temperature Reconstructions for the Last 2,000 Years.* Washington, DC: National Academy Press.

O'Sullivan, E. (1999) *Transformative Learning: Educational vision for the 21st century.* London: Zed Books.

Ofsted. (2008) *Schools and Sustainability: A climate for change?* London: Crown Copyright.

Orr, D. (1994) *Earth in Mind.* New York: First Island Press.

Orr, D. (2009) *Down to the Wire. Confronting climate collapse.* Oxford: Oxford University Press.

Oxfam (2009) Source http://southasia.oneworld.net/globalheadlines/ millions-hungry-due-to-climate-change-says-oxfam (accessed July 2009).

Pearce, J. C. (1998) 'Waking up to the holographic heart. Starting over with education', http://www.ratical.org/many_worlds/JCP98.html (accessed 22 July 2010).

Pearce, J. C. (2002) *The Crack in the Cosmic Egg: New Constructs Of Mind And Reality.* San Francisco: HarperCollins.

Peterson, T. C. (2008) 'State of the Climate in 2008, Special Supplement', *Bulletin of the American Meteorological Society* 90(8): S17–S18.

Porritt, J. (2009) *Living Within our Means: Avoiding the ultimate recession.* London: Forum for the Future.

Prochnik, G. (2010) *In Pursuit of Silence.* New York: Doubleday.

Putnam, R. D. (2000) *Bowling Alone. The collapse and revival of American community.* New York: Simon and Schuster.

Ramaswamy, V. (2006) 'Anthropogenic and natural influences in the evolution of lower stratospheric cooling', *Science* 311: 138–114.

Rees, M. (2003) *Our Final Century.* London: Arrow Books.

Register, R. (2006) *Ecocities: Rebuilding cities in balance with nature.* Gabriola Island, BC: New Society Publishers.

Reimer, E. (1971) *School is Dead. An essay on alternatives in education.* Harmondsworth: Penguin.

Reynolds, D., Sammons, P., De Fraine, B., Townsend, T. and Van Damme, J. (2011) 'Educational Effectiveness Research (EER): A State of the Art Review'. Paper presented to the annual meeting of the International Congress for School Effectiveness and Improvement, Cyprus, 2011.

Ridley, M. (2010) *The Rational Optimist.* London: HarperCollins.

Rogers, R. (1997) *Cities for a Small Planet.* London: Faber and Faber.

Ruskin, J. (1864–1865) 'Sesame and Lilies', a lecture series given at Rusholme, Manchester.

Sankara, T. (1985) *Thomas Sankara Speaks: The Burkina Faso Revolution 1983– 1987* (trans. Samantha Anderson). New York: Pathfinder.

Santer, B. D. (1996) 'A search for human influences on the thermal structure of the atmosphere', *Nature* 382: 39–46.

Santer, B. D. (2003), 'Contributions of anthropogenic and natural forcing to recent tropopause height changes', *Science* 301: 479–483.

Sarason, S. (1993) *The Predictable Failure of Educational Reform: Can we change course before it's too late?* San Francisco: Jossey–Bass.

Scharmer, C. O. (2008) *Theory U. Learning from the future as it emerges.* San Francisco, CA: Berrett Koehler Publishers.

Scheffer, M. (2009). *Critical Transitions in Nature and Society.* Princeton, NJ: Princeton University Press.

Schumacher, E. F. (1973) *Small is Beautiful. Economics as if people mattered.* London: HarperBusiness.

Scott, W. and Gough, S. (2003). *Sustainable Development and Learning: Framing the issues.* London: Taylor & Francis.

Sen, A. (1999) *Development as Freedom.* Oxford: Oxford University Press.

Senge, P., Scharmer, C. O., Jaworski, J. and Flowers, B. (2004) *Presence: Human purpose, and the field of the future.* Cambridge, MA: Society for Organizational Learning.

Shimizu, M., Takami, Y., Adachi, K., Ogino, N. and Tanaka, H. (2002) 'A Study of the Effect of the "Forest Mulle Activity" on Environmental Learning at Schools in Japan'. Abstract published in *Skogsmullesymposium Journal* 2002, Lidingö.

Soros, G. (2008) *The New Paradigm for Financial Markets.* New York: Public Affairs Books.

Steel, C. (2009) *Hungry City: How food shapes our lives.* London: Vintage.

Sterling, S. (2001) 'Sustainable Education: Re-visioning learning and change', *Schumacher Briefings 6.* Bristol: Green Books.

Tilbury, D. (2011) *Education for Sustainable Development: An expert review of processes and learning.* Paris: UNESCO.

UNESCO (2009) *Learning for a Sustainable World: Review of contexts and structures for ESD.* Paris: UNESCO.

United Nations (1987) 'Report of the World Commission on Environment and Development: Our Common Future', Annex to A/42/427 (Development and International Co-operation: Environment Bruntland Commission).

United Nations (1987) 'Report of the World Commission on Environment and Development', General Assembly Resolution 42/187, 11th December 1987.

United Nations Population Predictions http://www.un.org/esa/population/publications/longrange2/WorldPop2300final.pdf (accessed 15th December 2010).

Wals, A. E. J. (2007) 'Learning in a changing world and changing in a learning world: reflexively fumbling towards sustainability', *Southern African Journal of Environmental Education* 24(1): 35–45.

Wals, A. E. J. and Blewitt, J. (2010). 'Third wave sustainability in higher education: Some (inter)national trends and developments', in P. Jones, D.

Selby and S. Sterling (eds), *Green Infusions: Embedding sustainability across the Higher Education curriculum*. London: Earthscan, pp. 55–74.

Waters, A. (2008) *Edible Schoolyard*. San Francisco, CA: Chronicle Books.

Wenger, E. (1998) *Communities of Practice*. Cambridge: Cambridge University Press.

Wenger, E., McDermott, R. and Snyder, W. (2002) *Cultivating Communities of Practice. A guide to managing knowledge*. Boston, MA: Harvard Business School.

White, J. A. and White, N. J. (2006), 'A 20th century acceleration in global sea level rise', *Geophysical Research Letters*, 33: L01602, doi:10.1029/2005GL024826. (The global sea level estimate described in this work can be downloaded from the CSIRO website.)

Wilson, E. O. (1991) *The Diversity of Life*. Harvard, CT: Harvard University Press.

Wilson, E. O. (2002) *The Future of Life*. Harvard, CT: Harvard University Press.

Index

Bold figures refer to figures and tables